W9-BWJ-296

Psi SEARCH

Norma Bowles
and
Fran Hynds

with
Joan Maxwell

Published in San Francisco by

Harper & Row, Publishers

New York   Hagerstown   San Francisco   London

Dedication

To scientists everywhere—including researchers into psi—who pose new questions of nature and who, rather than making data fit inadequate theories, are willing to live with ambiguity.

Norma Bowles
Fran Hynds

Photo Credits

p. 1: Luisa Kolla Bowles, p. 6: Delmar Watson, p. 8: Delmar Watson, p. 10: Foundation for Research on the Nature of Man, p. 19: George R. Clovie, p. 23: Michal Heron, p. 21: George R. Clovie, p. 27: John Cutten, p. 28: Foundation for Research on the Nature of Man, p. 30 (bottom): Foundation for Research on the Nature of Man, p. 32: Foundation for Research on the Nature of Man, p. 37: Mark Handler, p. 36 Luisa Kolla Bowles, p. 38: Psychical Research Foundation, p. 39: Foundation for Research on the Nature of Man, p. 40: Psychical Research Foundation, p. 42: Oakland Tribune, p. 43: Charles Tart, p. 45 (top): Marcia Keegan, p. 45 (bottom): Ingo Swann, p. 47: Marcia Keegan, p. 48: John Farina, p. 50: Stuart Blue Harary, p. 51: Holsinger Studio, Charlottesville, W. Va., p. 54: Delmar Watson, p. 55: Stanford Research Institute, p. 57: Michael Ostovich, p. 15: American Society for Psychical Research, p. 59 (top): Marcia Keegan, p. 61: Houston Chronicle, p. 58: Marcia Keegan, p. 63 (right): Edgar D. Mitchell, *Psychic Exploration: A Challenge for Science* (New York: G. P. Putnam), p. 63 (left): Judy Tart, p. 65 (top): Marcia Keegan, p. 65 (bottom): Don Richards, p. 66: Stanford Research Institute, p. 67: Shipi Shtrang, Kadima Productions, Inc. p. 50: Russell Targ and Harold Puthoff, *Mind Reach* (New York: Delacorte Press), p. 76: Psychical Research Foundation, p. 77: Psychical Research Foundation, p. 78: Psychical Research Foundation, p. 81: Dave Techter, p. 85: Dave Techter, p. 87: Dave Techter, p. 86: Delmar Watson, p. 88: John Cutten, p. 90: Angus McBean, Parapsychology Foundation, p. 94: Delmar Watson, p. 95: Delmar Watson, p. 97 (top): Dub Allen, p. 97 (bottom): Dr. Thomas Budzynski, p. 98: Menninger Foundation, p. 99: James L. Hickman, p. 100: Thelma Moss, p. 102: George Harrison, p. 104: J. G. Pratt, p. 105: Colorado State Historical Society and KOA-TV, p. 106: Jule Eisenbud, p. 107: Colorado State Historical Society and KOA-TV, p. 109: Delmar Watson, p. 111 (top): Lee Magid, p. 111 (bottom): William Lear, p. 112: Jet Propulsion Lab, California Institute of Technology, p. 113 (top): L. H. Walter, p. 113 (bottom): Thelma Moss, p. 114: Ampex Corp., p. 115: Photo by E. H. Kanzelmyer, Courtesy of Grace B. Kanzelmyer, p. 117: Photo by E. H. Kanzelmyer, Courtesy of Grace B. Kanzelmyer, p. 116: American Society of Dowsers, Inc., p. 119: Doubleday, p. 125: Dave Techter, p. 124: Robert Van de Castle, p. 126 (left): Edgar Cayce Foundation, p. 128: Human Dimensions Institute, p. 129: Marcia Keegan, p. 130: Mark Handler, p. 131: Sally Young.

Designed by Fifth Street Design Associates

Library of Congress Cataloging in Publication Data

Bowles, Norma.
   Psi search.

   Bibliography: p.
     1. Psychical research. I. Hynds, Fran, joint author.
II. Maxwell, Joan, joint author. III. Title.
BF1031.B718   1978   133.8   77-21072
ISBN 0-06-064083-9

78 79 80 81 82 10 9 8 7 6 5 4 3 2

Contents

Prefatory Statement

The subject of psychic phenomena has long been controversial and confused. In this book, *Psi SEARCH*, the authors render a useful public service by calling attention to the need to distinguish information which has been scientifically demonstrated in the laboratory from the many other kinds of material popularly associated with psychic phenomena.

Margaret Mead
Glenn Seaborg

Acknowledgments

This book, *Psi SEARCH*, is the result of a huge and sustained volunteer effort. Hundreds of scientists and other volunteers—both professional and lay persons—made it possible. They cannot all be individually thanked, for that would be a book in itself. Instead, the following credits have been prepared and, as most of them are only partial lists, it is hoped that everyone else who served will know how sincerely their contribution is appreciated.

Psi SEARCH Advisors
The largest debt is owed to three distinguished scientists: Dr. Stanley Krippner, Program Planning Coordinator, Humanistic Psychology Institute; Dr. Robert Morris, Lecturer, Tutorial Program, University of California at Santa Barbara; and Dr. Robert Van de Castle, Department of Psychiatry, University of Virginia Medical School, who unstintingly gave of their valuable time to review and sift experiments, read draft after draft of manuscript, and answer untold questions in response to frantic telephone calls. They represented the official cooperation of their professional organization—the Parapsychological Association (P.A.).

Special Mentors
Special gratitude is owed Dr. J. B. Rhine, the eminent parapsychologist who founded the Parapsychology Laboratory at Duke University and later, the Foundation for Research on the Nature of Man (FRNM) at Durham, North Carolina. Dr. Rhine read sections of this book in manuscript and patiently answered dozens of questions from the authors. His broad support of the Psi SEARCH effort has been especially valued.

Of great benefit was the generous counsel of Dr. K. Ramakrishna Rao, Professor of Psychology at Andhra University, Waltair, India (presently Director of the Research Institute of the FRNM). Substantial and frequent assistance came from other researchers:

William G. Braud, Ph.D.
Mind Science Foundation
San Antonio, Texas

Douglas Dean
Newark College of Engineering
Newark, New Jersey

Jule Eisenbud, M.D.
Denver, Colorado

Charles Honorton
Maimonides Medical Center
Brooklyn, New York

Edward Kelly,
Dept. of Electrical Engineering
Duke University

Seymour Mauskopf, Ph.D.
Duke University
Durham, North Carolina

Karlis Osis, Ph.D.
American Society for Psychical Research
New York, New York

J. G. Pratt, Ph.D.
University of Virginia School of Medicine
Charlottesville, Virginia

Harold Puthoff, Ph.D.
Stanford Research Institute
Menlo Park, California

Louisa E. Rhine, Ph.D.
Foundation for Research on the
 Nature of Man
Durham, North Carolina

William Roll
Psychical Research Foundation
Durham, North Carolina

Gertrude Schmeidler, Ph.D.
City College of the
 City University of New York
New York, New York

Helmut Schmidt, Ph.D.
Mind Science Foundation
San Antonio, Texas

Rex Stanford, Ph.D.
Center for Parapsychological Research
Austin, Texas

Ian Stevenson, M.D.
University of Virginia School of Medicine
Charlottesville, Virginia

Charles Tart, Ph.D.
University of California
Davis, California

And Psi SEARCH owes much to the writings of the eminent American psychologist Gardner Murphy.

A Partial List of Sources of Information and Assistance

In addition to the articles and research of all the persons already named, there were many other individuals and a number of organizations that provided essential information and materials:

Alan Angoff
John Artly, Ph.D.
John Beloff, Ph.D.
Hans Bender, Ph.D.
Lendell W. Braud, Ph.D.
David Bresler, Ph.D.
Barbara Brown, Ph.D.
Thomas Budzynski, Ph.D.
James Carpenter, Ph.D.
Manfred Cassirer
Hugh Lynn Cayce
W. E. Cox
Henry Dakin
James Davis
Pamela de Maigret
Sally Ann Drucker
Yvonne Duplessis, Ph.D.
Norman Emerson, Ph.D.
Jeff Eriksen
Jarl Ingmar Fahler
R. Buckminster Fuller
Jeffrey Goodman
Bernard Grad, Ph.D.
Jo Marie Haight
Stuart Blue Harary
Sharon Harper
Arthur Hastings, Ph.D.
Gerald Jampolsky, M.D.
Martin Johnson, Ph.D.
H. K. Kanthamani, Ph.D.
Pascal Kaplan, Ph.D.
Shafica Karagulla, M.D.
Jim Kennedy
Judith Klein

Dolores Krieger, Ph.D.
Ronald Lippitt, Ph.D.
Edwin C. May, Ph.D.
Edgar Mitchell, Sc.D.
Thelma Moss, Ph.D.
William McGarey, M.D.
Michael McVaugh, Ph.D.
C. B. Nash, Ph.D.
Robert Nelson
Dennis O'Brien
Brendan O'Regan
John Palmer, Ph.D.
H. H. Rao
Zdenck Rejdak, Ph.D.
David Rogers, Ph.D.
D. Scott Rogo
Milan Ryzl, Ph.D.
Eva Schlinder-Rainman, D.S.W.
Harold Sherman
Eloise Shields
Sister Mary Justa Smith, Ph.D.
Gerald Solfvin
Ingo Swann
Russell Targ
Judy Taddonio, Ph.D.
James Terry
William A. Tiller, Ph.D.
Montague Ullman, M.D.
Anita M. Watkins
Graham M. Watkins
Roger Wells
John White

American Society of Dowsers, Inc.
Danville, Vermont

American Society for Psychical Research
New York, New York

Art Center College of Design
Pasadena, California

A.R.E. Clinic, Inc.
Virginia Beach, Virginia and
    Phoenix, Arizona

Foundation for Parasensory Investigation
(now called Foundation for Inner Peace)
New York, New York

Institute Metapsychique International
Paris, France

Institute of Noetic Sciences
Palo Alto, California

Institute for Parapsychology, Foundation
for Research on the Nature of Man
Durham, North Carolina

ISHI Research Center for
  Consciousness Studies
Cambridge, Massachusetts

Mankind Research Foundation
Washington, D.C.

Mind Science Foundation
San Antonio, Texas

Philosophical Research Society
Los Angeles, California

Parapsychology Foundation
New York, New York

Psychical Research Foundation
Durham, North Carolina

Southern California Society for
  Psychical Research
Los Angeles, California

Research Coordinators

Coordinating the research was a team headed by James Hickman, technical director, and Joanna Morris, literary advisor, and including Mary Lou Carlson, John Hubbacher, David Phillips, Joseph Rush, Allayne Scott.

The Exhibition as a Sounding Board to Public Response

This book, based on an exhibition, was possible only because of the creative vision and unflagging support of the California Museum of Science and Industry. Most especially to be thanked is its Director, William J. McCann, who welcomed the production of an exhibition on psychic phenomena. Richard Byrne, Associate Dean of the Annenberg School of Communications at the University of Southern California, deserves special credit for designing the exhibition under very difficult circumstances.

  With the circulation of Psi SEARCH through the Smithsonian Institution Traveling Exhibition Service, the exhibition was viewed by 1½ million people, and invaluable material about the nature of the public interest and response to the subject was collected for this book.

Patrons and Sponsors

The credibility of the Psi SEARCH presentations —to which the authority of this book is owed—was sustained by the reviews made regularly by successive Councils of the Parapsychological Association from 1974–77. Their encouragement has been greatly appreciated. The warm reception of Psi SEARCH amongst scientists and educators generally can be attributed to its sponsorship by an-

thropologist Margaret Mead, Nobel Laureate Glenn T. Seaborg, and their various committees. Three educators in particular have given Psi SEARCH their valued attention: Glenn Olds, Joseph Platt, and Terry Sanford.

A Partial List of Supporters

A period of five years passed while the Psi SEARCH approach of investigating and reporting on psychic phenomena was evolving into a book. Throughout that time, literally hundreds of other people added their expertise and financial support to the endeavor. Foremost among these were:

Edward Armfield
Anna Bing Arnold
Winifred Babcock
Marion and Alphonzo Bell
James Bolen
Hargrove Bowles
Suzanne Bush
Geraldine Cassidy
Hugh Chatham
Eileen Coly
Beverly Copeland
Debbie Dawson
Henry Drake
Arrolla DuBridge
Robert Froeber
Jerome Frank
Toni Frank
Lois Gaines
Betty Jane Gerber
Ruth Gluck
Linda Hagans
Eileen Harakel
David Hammond
Frank Hanes
Jesse Helms
Bud Hopps
Laura Huxley
Larry and Belle James
Ray Johnson
Joan Kaiser
Richard Kauffman
Donald Keene
Fanny Knipe
Lucy Mack
Irene March-Davison
John McCarty
Pat McGuire
Meg McDonald
Donna Medrano
Jack Mitchell

Harry Mullens
Evelyn DeWolfe Nadel
Marian Nester
Mary and Charles Neff
Sue Oliver
Legory O'Loughlin
Jane Otto
Ruth Peale
Maxwell Perrow
Charles Pigg
Hasel Popják
Richardson Preyer
Rosa Lee Proby
Ted Rockwell
Jeanne Scott
Judy Skutch
Jean and Robert Sprague
Eleanor Wasson
Greta Waingrow
Patty and Don Westerbeke
Liz White
Nancy Williams
Fran Brown Zeff
Howard Zimmerman

Reserved for the Last
Deeply personal and warm appreciation goes to: the Kolla-Landwehr Foundation for funding this undertaking; the individual members of the Bowles and Hynds families for their loving concern, patience, and encouragement; Joan Maxwell, professional writer, who blended our different styles of writing and divergent viewpoints into a single voice.

And a final appreciation is hereby expressed for the special contribution provided by the loyal opposition: the skeptics, who continue to challenge all of us into examining psychic phenomena as conservatively, as carefully, and as thoughtfully as possible.

Norma Bowles
Fran Hynds

October 18, 1977

I.

Beginnings of the Search

Since the beginning of recorded history, people have been perplexed by personal experiences in which they dream about events that later occur, know what another person is thinking without being told, perceive events that happen too far away to be seen, or influence something solely by an exercise of their minds. Experimental investigation of these unusual occurrences leads the scientists who study them to hypothesize an unknown factor underlying all of them. They call this factor **psi**.

Psi, the twenty-third letter of the Greek alphabet, is often used in scientific equations to stand for the unknown. When used in connection with psychic occurrences, psi represents a mystery that, after fifty years of laboratory study, one hundred years of scientific investigation, and centuries of great popular interest, remains unsolved.

1.
The Circle of
Confusion

"I went to this psychic last week and he was wonderful. He told me exactly what was going to happen in my life."

"Psychic phenomena? That's only for people who'll believe anything. There's nothing to it that can't be explained by coincidence."

"What's this p . . . s . . . i, anyway?"

These three remarks offer a small sampling of the widely divergent reactions we encountered when we began our investigation of psychic phenomena. Why is the subject so controversial? Is there anything to it? What is the truth behind all the stories we hear?

We have spent five years seeking answers to these questions, evaluating material from a great variety of sources, and sifting conflicting opinions. We produced a museum exhibit on psychic phenomena based on what we learned. Since then we learned still more about this provocative and complex subject, and so have come to write this book.

Throughout this search for answers about psi, we have become profoundly aware of how inextricably the subject of psychic phenomena is associated with a wide-ranging mass of esoteric, metaphysical, and occult belief. We have come to recognize how most people lump together into their ideas of psychic phenomena almost anything and everything unexplained, from astrology to unidentified flying objects. In the midst of all this confusion about psi, we have come to see manifold inaccuracies, exaggerations, and misrepresentations. These, we think, created much of the mystery in the first place, generating an escalating spiral of confusion from early times to the present day.

When we set out on our search, we had no idea we were stepping blithely into quicksand. We were blissfully unaware that trustworthy information about psychic phenomena would be so hard to find. Perhaps we were fortunate, for if we had known what we were getting into, we might never have begun.

Our first step in this investigative effort was to seek advice from friends and acquaintances who were scientists. We knew that some laboratory experimental investigation of psychic phenomena had been done and assumed these scientists could lead us to the experts in the field.

We were wrong. A former science advisor to a president of the United States said he had looked at the first published ESP test reports in 1934, had found them unimpressive, and had not

The Scientific Method

The distinguished philosopher Bertrand Russell had this to say about the scientific method:

> . . . although in its more refined forms, it may seem complicated, (the scientific method) is in essence remarkably simple. It consists in observing such facts as will enable the observer to discover general laws governing facts of the kind in question. The two stages, first of observation, and second of inference to a law, are both essential, and each is susceptible of almost indefinite refinement; but in essence the first man who said "fire burns" was employing scientific method, at any rate if he had allowed himself to be burnt several times. This man had already passed through the two stages of observation and generalization. He had not, however, what scientific technique demands—a careful choice of significant facts on the one hand, and, on the other hand, various means of arriving at laws otherwise than by mere generalization . . .*

---

*Bertrand Russell, *The Scientific Outlook*. (London: George Allen & Unwin, Ltd., 1931) p.15

pursued the subject further. A distinguished husband and wife team of psychologists, experienced in the design of scientific exhibits, said it would be impossible to make an exhibit on the scientific findings about psi. Like the Emperor's new suit of clothes, they said, there was simply nothing there. A Nobel laureate in physics told us the psi field was typical of so-called soft sciences, which make untenable claims based on insufficient evidence. The only thought a renowned neurobiologist would share with us was that it could be dangerous for the public to have information about psi.

Thus our original plan to locate expert assistance failed. We were discouraged to find that our scientific friends could provide us none. We were more at sea than ever—without a conceptual framework of any kind to guide us. And the quest almost ended before it began.

When we widened our search, we soon discovered a plethora of "authorities". There were, we found, an almost endless number of people and groups who have become involved with psychic phenomena. Most of them espouse some deeply held bias about the subject, and many of them contradict each other.

Eventually we found the expert assistance we sought, but only after we had rummaged around a lot on our own. We studied the subject via many routes: a UCLA seminar on unorthodox methods of healing, a course on higher sense perception, a mind control methodology designed to increase our alpha brain waves, pyramid power experimentation, the mystical teachings of Blavatsky, a regressions expert, and a Theosophical seance. We spoke with a businessman named Don Westerbeke from San Francisco about the psychic surgery he had undergone in the Philippines, and heard the head of the department of material sciences at a major university discourse on his mathematics of evolving consciousness. We met with journalist Virginia Stombough, who described the games she had devised to teach children how to see auras. We heard a teacher of mind control explain that he had been so frightened by the unusual disturbances experienced by his advanced students that he was giving up the class.

During all this exploration, we were bombarded by anecdotes about apparent spontaneous psychic occurrences in daily life. An elderly woman described seeing her son standing at the foot of her bed at the moment of his death three hundred miles away; a man told us of a real-life experience in which he felt he had looked down at his own blood-spattered body lying unconscious in a ditch after an automobile crash; a child described misdialing a telephone number and as a result saving the life of a stranger suffering a heart attack.

We found these stories and others like them fascinating. Early psi researchers, equally intrigued by similar reports, filled the journals of the British and American Societies for Psychical Research with well over one thousand different accounts of apparent psi occurrences. In fact, present-day researchers still collect and examine psi stories. Yet while spontaneous incidents constitute an exciting part of the story of psi, we found that they are impossible to evaluate.

Consider, for example, the following incident, told to us by a college sophomore:

> It happened when I was still in high school. It was Sunday, and I had been out partying the night before, and I came home really late. My mom let me sleep all that morning because I had been out so late.
>
> I woke up in the early afternoon from a terrible nightmare. We live in a two-story house, and I dreamed I was talking with my mom on the landing at the top of the stairs when the front door opened, my pop came in from playing golf, put his golf bag down on the stairs, and fell down dead from a heart attack.
>
> I was so upset by the dream that I ran out of my room to find my mom. She was just coming up the stairs and we stood on the top landing while I told her my dream about how pop died. Just as I finished telling her, the front door opened. It was my pop, coming home from playing golf. He put his golf bag down on the stairs and fell down dead from a heart attack, just like in the dream.

Although we found her story—which she told with great feeling—very moving, we were unable to find objective proof that the things she described had actually happened in just that way. Perhaps her memory of that emotionally shattering experience differed from what had really happened. Perhaps she was simply trying to gain attention and sympathy. Or perhaps she was telling the exact, unvarnished truth. As was true of all the other stories we heard, we could not verify her report.

We kept coming back again and again to a need for objective information, a way to assess material about psi for the public. As we had known from the beginning, there is a field of science—known as parapsychology—engaged in the investigation of psychic phenomena. We decided to take a second, in-depth look at the field despite the repeated warnings of leading scientists that we would be wasting our time. This time we went not to scientists in other disciplines but instead directly to scientists actively engaged in parapsychological research.

We found there are only a relative handful of scientists investigating psychic phenomena, which may explain why their work is so little known. Yet sound scientific work by competent investigators has been going on in research laboratories for over fifty years. Furthermore, thanks to some new techniques, in the last few years researchers have answered a number of perplexing and fundamental questions about the subject. The most reliable reports of this fascinating work are published in scientific professional journals.

While we certainly do not consider the information contained in professional journal articles to be infallible, we believe that it offers the best available way to separate demonstrated facts from the unproven speculation surrounding psi. We know that many people believe no true understanding of psi will ever be reached by the scientific method alone. We certainly are not wed to the idea that the scientific method is the only means of perceiving reality. But after encountering so much confusion about psi, we find the scientific method's concern for objectivity and logical analysis of enormous value. At least it could be helpful if more

The Scientific Method and Professional Journals

The facts published in the professional journals have been obtained through the scientific method of inquiry. The practice of encouraging scientists to repeat experiments done by others to see whether or not similar results are obtained seems to be one of the scientific method's main strengths. Publication encourages the elimination of intentional or unintentional errors of testing and analysis and also encourages other experimenters to retest the findings.

Six major English-language professional journals, affiliated with the Parapsychological Association, are published for the benefit of scientists engaged in research concerning psychic phenomena. These journals provide authoritative information about past and present laboratory research on psi. (For their addresses, see the Appendix.) They are:

International Journal of Parapsychology (IJP)
Journal of Parapsychology (JP)
Journal of the American Society for Psychical Research (JASPR)
Journal of the Society for Psychical Research (JSPR)
Research in Parapsychology (RIP)
European Journal of Parapsychology (EJP)

These journals are written and edited by scientists for scientists. Each article's results have been thoroughly evaluated by one or more scientific reviewers before publication to verify that correct scientific procedure has been followed.

The professional publications in which professional psi investigators publish the results of their scientific research.

people were aware that extensive scientific investigation of psi
has taken place. But few people are.

From our own experience in reading the journals, we can easily
understand why the general public knows so little about the
scientific findings. Researchers in parapsychology describe their
findings in complex, technical, almost incomprehensible reports
and publish them in highly specialized, hard-to-locate journals. It
is not the kind of literature one keeps on the bedside table!

As a result of preparing the museum exhibit, and then following it as it traveled across the United States and Canada, we have
had the chance to learn how people really feel about psychic
phenomena. One thing we can testify to is that few are neutral.
Their opinions on the subject are as varied as the fish in the sea.

Some share our hunger for objective information. Others prefer
the esoteric and are fascinated by Kirlian photography, magic
mushrooms, or ways to learn how to have ESP.

For many, the more mystery the better. A young taxi driver who
drove us from the airport to a museum in the Midwest announced
that he was fascinated by psi. As evidence of psychic phenomena,
he folded a piece of paper, cut it, and showed that the pieces could
then be arranged to spell the word *hell* and also to take the shape of
a cross. When we asked how that provided evidence of psi, he
replied, "Obviously it's evidence of psychic phenomena—it's
unexplainable, isn't it?"

Others rely on preconceived ideas about psi based on their particular belief systems. (This approach is discussed at length in the next chapter.) For example, when those who believe in life after death think they have seen a ghost, they are convinced that they have seen evidence of the after-life; no other explanation seems possible. On one specific occasion, we heard a self-styled expert persist in asserting that all psi is explained by the human pineal gland, which he firmly knew to be "the third eye." And if such people find it hard to give up their preconceptions, preferring them to contradictory theories, they can scarcely be blamed. Psi concepts appear to relate to time and space, miraculous healing, and many other of life's most profound questions.

Skeptics, we have noticed, are apt to have a similar difficulty with psychic phenomena. Once they have made up their minds that common sense rules out psi's existence, they tend to deny the validity of any laboratory evidence to the contrary.

Then there are the thrill-seekers. We heard a presumably serious educator interrupt an advanced symposium on psi research to ask one of the speakers what he knew about messages from what he called "ascending beings." Many people demand the entire subject of psychic phenomena be spectacular. They feel cheated when it isn't. A TV interviewer was incredulous when she discovered we expected to discuss scientific findings about the subject. She had planned that we would entertain her morning television audience with parlor tricks. "Oh, come now," she kept urging us, "do something psi."

The temptation for the media to satisfy the public thirst for the sensational is never greater than in this remarkable field, and who is to reprimand them when the real facts are so few and far between? We were asked to preview a feature-length film on psychic phenomena for general audiences. We were astounded to find that it would be released, even though it contained over one hundred specific inaccuracies and a basic point of view that was grossly misleading, all of which had been pointed out to the producer.

We will never forget another instance of a program dealing with psi that went astray. Some parapsychology buffs had led the cameramen from a local TV station in a real-life attempt to exorcise a poltergeist agent in someone's home. The misfortune for us was that the episode was viewed by an administrative member of a major university who had been warming toward giving us some advice for our project. His sensibilities were outraged by the questionable program, and he cooled considerably toward the whole topic of psi. This we found to be typical of the way sensationalism can prevent someone from becoming seriously interested in the field.

And we further observed that the passionate preoccupation with which some people embrace psi can often be as detrimental as sensationalism when it comes to winning new friends from among cautious people. On one occasion people's over-enthusiasm closed down our exhibit. The director of a local science museum that was presenting Psi SEARCH abruptly terminated the exhibit early. It seems that, in response to the exhibit, a number of psychic buffs had quite vociferously volunteered

Margaret Mead, the internationally renowned anthropologist, who served (with Glenn Seaborg) as co-chairperson of the Psi SEARCH exhibit.

their services as self-proclaimed authorities to speak on psi. The director, intimidated, apparently decided it would be safest simply to shut down the exhibit.

We found, too, that there are some people who would have a considerable adjustment to make in their professional life if they were to accept psi. A university professor told a group of parapsychologists with whom he was visiting that he had a ten-year research project underway and had already completed seven years of work on it. "If what you say about psi is true," he told them, "all of those seven years will be wasted. It will take a lot more evidence to convince me."

We soon learned that it was impossible to stereotype how any one group might respond. For instance, some people from various religious denominations are convinced that any investigation of psychic phenomena is a form of blasphemy. On the other hand, others from these same denominations, often including the clergy themselves, praise the research as a further indication that human beings are created in the image and likeness of God.

In the midst of these divergent opinions, our job was to prepare an unbiased report distinguishing between material that is scientific and material that is pseudoscientific or nonscientific. Locating the journals as a best possible resource was only a first step. We needed experts to work with us if we were to create a truly cautious, conservative, and credible presentation.

To solve that dilemma, we set out to enlist the cooperation of the Parapsychological Association (P.A.) in reviewing what we did. This organization is to psi research what the American Psychological Association is to psychology. Only with its professional assistance could we hope to evaluate, sift, and order the clearest and most representative information about psi from the mountains of journal articles that confronted us.

When we first thought of contacting the P.A., a number of people tried to discourage us. They said, "You will find them reticent and unwilling to cooperate." And in fact, their initial attitude towards us was stand-offish; they declined our original invitation to participate in the museum exhibit. As we came to know the researchers better, we learned the reasons for their reluctance. Their work has frequently been abused. Commercial interests try to exploit it and often succeed. Their findings are often misrepresented, their research sometimes assailed. But they were eventually won over by our resolve to focus on experimental findings published in scientific journals.

Three distinguished scientists, representing the P.A., helped research, screen, select, revise, and approve the museum exhibit. Five signatures in all appeared on every page of the final presentation. The efforts of our advisors represent the first joint evaluation of psi for the general public ever attempted by active researchers, and this book contains the fruits of those efforts.

We hope that the conceptual framework provided by this book, reflected in its basic effort to distinguish scientific data from all other kinds of investigation, will make it easier for the reader to evaluate this complex and controversial subject. To that end, information about psi that has been demonstrated in the laboratory is grouped in a section called Psi. Information that may be

The Parapsychological Association

Formed in 1957, the Parapsychological Association (P.A.) is made up of biologists, chemists, engineers, mathematicians, physicists, psychologists, psychiatrists, and other scientists engaged in psi research. The P.A. is the only international association of psi researchers. It was admitted into membership in the august American Association for the Advancement of Science in 1969.

When the American Association for the Advancement of Science was debating whether or not to admit the P.A. to membership, the P.A.'s cause was advanced by Margaret Mead. In the course of her persuasive argument in its favor, she said, "For the last ten years we have been arguing about what constitutes science and scientific method and what societies use it. We even changed the by-laws about it. The P.A. uses statistics and blinds, placebos, double blinds and other standard scientific devices. The whole history of scientific advancement is full of scientists investigating phenomena that the establishment did not believe were there. I submit that we vote in favor of this association's work."

And they did.

The founders of the Parapsychological Association, the only international professional organization of researchers into psychic phenomena.

psi-related, but has not yet been fully tested in the laboratory, can be found in a section called SEARCH. Psi and SEARCH taken together provide what we believe is a reasonably accurate picture of psi at the present time.

The current status of psi reminds us of some of the charming stories of Benjamin Franklin's electrical showmanship. In addition to flying kites decked with keys during thunderstorms, Franklin amused himself and his friends by electrically ringing bells and making metals glow and wires dance. Once he even used an electrical charge to ignite some rum. Casual passersby gawked through his garden fence at his electrical pranks, but none of the watchers, not even Franklin himself, could imagine how profoundly his new and delightful toy would eventually transform the way people live. Looking at psi today, we wonder if its effect on future generations may not rival or even surpass the effect of electricity on our own.

It is because of the possibility of such a prospect that we welcome you to join with us in the search for psi.

2.
Obstacles to Objectivity

Any search for psi encounters severe complications in the form of a number of factors peculiar to the phenomenon. These factors make it remarkably difficult for anyone to remain objective about psi. One of the biggest obstacles to objectivity comes from the very nature of psi itself.

The qualities attributed to psi resemble qualities most people have reserved for deities, not humans. Omniscience—knowing everything, the past, the future, even the deepest secret hidden in a human heart—and omnipotence—power over everything, the ability to influence events at will—these two qualities have customarily been ascribed only to heavenly beings. Now, as will be seen in the following chapters, laboratory research into psi has shown that humans may possess powers that partake of both omniscience and omnipotence. The ability to read another's thoughts, to foretell the future, and to see things happening too far away to be seen, are three aspects of omniscience. The ability to influence the environment through the force of one's mind alone resembles godlike powers more closely than it does traditional human powers. Yet, with psi, it appears that humans can do these things.

A second problem has to do with confusion between psi and the occult. Early ritualistic practices in both magic and religion attempted to obtain knowledge about the future and to foster events that would be beneficial to the practitioner. Many peoples of Africa and Western Asia attempted to divine the future through rituals involving earth or sand. A number of prehistoric cave paintings and tribal dances may have been attempts to ensure a successful hunt. The ancient Greeks consulted oracles, as did peoples in China, Hawaii, and the Americas.

All these peoples were searching for help in matters of the utmost importance to them. They were groping for ways to control their world or to predict the future. Because of the importance they attached to these practices, they shrouded their rituals in great secrecy. Rites were hedged in totem and taboo, limited to initiates, and passed along to only a selected few.

Along with such official practices, various cultures evolved a number of more dubious rituals. Their practitioners wrapped themselves in the same secrecy and mystery associated with the more accepted rites. Witches announced their powers to curse or to cure, cults met in the dark hours of the night, special groups united to practice black magic. These practices, and others not quite so suspect, form a body of tradition known as the occult. They, too, attempt to provide their followers with pathways to omniscience and omnipotence.

And this has caused problems. Many people associate systems of occultism with psi because these systems attempt to deal with some of the same abilities psi does. In consequence, many view psi with the same suspicion and skepticism as they do the occult. The confusion between parapsychology and the occult is so strong in the public mind that, as the British parapsychologist G.N.M. Tyrrell has written, scientists ". . . are afraid that the least display of interest or acquiescence on their part [in parapsychology] may promote a great outburst of superstition on the part of the public, a relapse into a belief in witchcraft, necromancy and the black arts in general. . . ."[2]

Stuart Holroyd agrees: "Why, then, is parapsychology about as suspect and unacceptable to the scientific community as a whole as psychical research was nearly a century ago? . . . Because it threatens to reinstitute the supernatural from which science only emancipated itself after a long struggle."[1]

In considering the special difficulties encountered by people studying psi, the writer D. Scott Rogo has observed, "Perhaps the most serious problem facing parapsychologists is that of fraud."[3] A number of people will untruthfully assert that they are able to harness their alleged psychic powers to perform certain tasks—which they will happily perform on demand, in exchange for a fee. Many a fortuneteller predicts the future in conveniently ambiguous terms. Some self-proclaimed mediums promise to bring the bereaved messages from the dead. Such fraudulent practices, designed only to part the unwary from their money, hark back to ancient times.

But the unscrupulous keep up with modern technology as well. One ingenious group recently announced that dangerous rays emanating from one's television set would destroy what some call the third eye and so wipe out viewers' psychic abilities. Fortunately, they added, they were able to prevent such a catastrophe. All fearful viewers needed to do was to purchase a small packet of herbs from the group and keep this packet between themselves and their television. Every dangerous ray would be captured by the herbs, the group asserted, and the viewers' psychic abilities would survive unscathed.

With so many dubious practices associated with psi, and for so long a period of time, it is not surprising that some people find it hard to view the field objectively.

Another obstacle to objectivity about psi is the profound emotional effect anecdotes of personal psychic experiences have on some listeners. As Mary Craig Sinclair, wife of the novelist Upton Sinclair, once commented, "The fact of telepathy is one of the most terrifying in existence."[4] Some find such stories thrilling, and some find them terrifying. Consider, for example, the following incident mentioned in passing to the authors by a gifted psychic.

She said that one day she and a friend who was also a sensitive found themselves waiting for a third friend to arrive. To pass the time, they amused themselves by placing pea-sized bits of cotton

An ancient Egyptian amulet purported to have "psychic powers" against misfortune.

on a table top and trying to move them by means of psi. According to the psychic, they succeeded. She painted a vivid picture of herself and her friend, sitting close together, hands in their laps, watching the cotton bits appear to jump and move in response to their will.

Reactions to this anecdote vary. Some find it fascinating and enticing, and want to try it themselves. Others reject it as nonsense, pointing out that the slightest current of air will move a bit of cotton.

Stories touching on more serious matters, such as life and death, call forth even stronger emotional reactions. One such story, also reported to the authors, involved a businessman who went to a party and, while at the dinner table, felt a cat repeatedly brushing itself against his leg. When he said to his host that he certainly had a most affectionate cat, the host laughed and replied, "But we have no cat in this house. You're imagining things." Eager to prove that his host was mistaken, the businessman pushed back his chair and looked on the floor—but no cat could be found. Nothing more out of the ordinary happened at the party, although the businessman noticed that the lady who was his dinner partner had grown quite pale and quiet.

A short time after the businessman returned home, he received a call from his dinner partner. She was crying. "You know that cat you felt at the table but couldn't find? Well, now I know why. When I got home I found a phone message that my father had just died. He always promised me that if he died he would send me a message through a cat. He died while we were having dinner, and the cat you thought you felt rubbing against your leg must have been the message he promised."

Neither of these anecdotes can be proven definitively. But what is particularly interesting about them in this context is the strong reactions they, as representative psi anecdotes, evoke from most people. Some accept them, some reject them, some want to know more. Whatever the reaction, it is strong—and strong emotions can sometimes cloud good judgment.

As the British psi critic D. J. West wrote, "It is quite obvious that this is a highly emotion-laden subject, and one that attracts cranks, dupes, and charlatans in embarrassing numbers. And it is from this unsavory crowd that the extrasensory experimenters have emerged. The field of extrasensory research remains a no-man's land between the lunatic fringe on the one hand and the academically unorthodox on the other."[5]

Another strong emotion evoked by the concept of psi is excitement. A number of scientists and others revel in the possibilities of psi. Some think psi may turn out to be the basic building block of human consciousness, in the same way that DNA appears to be one of the basic building blocks of the human body. Other researchers wonder if psi may not be the ultimate link between bodies and minds, a kind of communications loop linking the material and the nonmaterial universe. Many humanists think psi may connect all existence, past, present, and future, living and dead, animate and inanimate. Some educators think psi may be a vehicle that will finally allow people to tap the part of their brains that currently appears to lie dormant and unused.

But psi is not all positive. Some theorists may be excited by its possibilities, but others are frightened. They see these possibilities as carrying with them huge responsibilities, responsibilities which may be too heavy to bear. They liken the investigation of psi to the development of the atom bomb. They point out that mastery of nuclear fission gave humanity great power, but people are still paying a price for that power that may turn out to be the highest price of all: the complete destruction of the planet Earth and all who live on it. They think the same may be true of psi.

There are those who fear further investigation of psi because they fear the way its powers may be misused by evil people. They liken psi to electricity, a neutral force, which can be used to fill a room with warm light in the middle of the night but which also can be used to electrocute an enemy. What is to stop spies from using ESP to read the state secrets hidden in diplomats' minds, or from using psychokinesis (PK) to change the direction of missiles in warfare?

Still others fear psi because they believe its attributes are too powerful for mere humans and must be reserved for a supreme being. As has been mentioned, psychic powers have historically been associated with sacred beings. Some believe these special powers should not be defiled by ordinary people, who do not have "adequate spiritual training" and will thus be tempted to misuse psi for personal gain.

Yet others fear psi because the best remembered and most often retold apparent psychic experiences concern something traumatic, such as a dream correctly predicting the death of a loved one. They ask what good can come out of seeing something awful that is going to happen and being unable to do anything about it.

Another reason some fear psi is that possible psi experiences often appear to violate the concepts they have come to depend upon as frames of reference about the universe. Their current understanding of the way the world works tells them that it is impossible to clearly perceive something that has not yet occurred or something going on in a distant place—and yet such things happen with psi. An *out-of-body experience* (OBE, pronounced oh–be), in which people feel as though they are seeing the world from a place outside their physical body, completely violates people's traditional understanding of their relationship to their bodies.

For example, take the possible out-of-body experience of a young Irish psi researcher who said he was in an automobile accident and suddenly discovered himself looking back 150 yards at his body lying mutilated where his auto had skidded into a viaduct. Apparent OBEs as startling as that are reported by quite ordinary people without any previous psychic experience. People who feel they have had such experiences, even unaccompanied by personal injury, often say they are left in a highly nervous state, disoriented as to time and place, and wondering if they have gone insane.

Some sensitives can enter an OBE state at will, as will be

Shamen undergo spiritual training to become healers.

14

described, but the price of this ability can be very high. One sensitive who has had numerous OBE experiences was most successful as a psi subject in the scientific laboratory shortly after she was released from a mental hospital. The inherent contradiction between what she had been told about the way the world worked and her own personal experience led her to have strong and unsettling feelings of fear and self-distrust. These were somewhat alleviated by the psychiatric help she received and by her encounters in the psi laboratory with researchers who took her claims seriously enough to study them.

The fact that psi violates currently accepted rules about the way the world works distresses many observers. G. N. M. Tyrrell writes that conventional scientists "... intuitively feel that the facts of psychical research will no more mix with the beliefs of common sense than will oil with water. . . . They fear that the dissonant facts, if admitted, will disrupt the scheme of the known and familiar."[6]

When things don't work the way they have always worked, many people become afraid. In the 1800s travelers found there were whole regions of the Ural Mountains where the needles of their normally reliable compasses would deviate erratically, leading them in bewildering circles. The experience of having compasses suddenly go berserk led to the development of elaborate superstitions about the region. Then the magnetic attraction of certain local mineral deposits called lodestones was discovered, solving the frightening mystery and allaying travelers' fears. Since psi is a powerful process that is not yet understood, many elaborate and frightening superstitions have grown up around it, which may be difficult to dismiss from some minds until the mystery of psi itself is solved. And while these superstitions linger, some people will find it extremely difficult to view psi with objectivity.

Fear is certainly an understandable response to the fact of psi. Psychologist Gardner Murphy observed, "In the history of discovery there has always been the blur and the horror of that which refuses to be assimilated; observations which, however carefully repeated and checked, fall into no predetermined place in the jigsaw puzzle which we conceive to be reason."[7]

A final factor that can distort people's views about psi involves another attribute of the phenomenon that evokes yet another emotional response—psi seduces. Psi seduces because of its subjective nature. Although many can be convinced of psi's presence only by some objective evidence, those who believe they have actually experienced psi can be so overwhelmed by the experience that any thought of objectivity or proof is quickly forgotten.

The strange power of psi over those who experience it can be compared to the enormous power of the experience of being in love. When little boys and girls go to the movies, they hoot scornfully at "all that kissing stuff," but not long afterward "all that kissing stuff" becomes the only way to behave, everything shines with a radiant light, and their beloved is the most wonderful person in the world. People who believe they have personally encountered psi assert that the power of psi, like the power of love,

Gardner Murphy of George Washington University, author of a number of works on psychology and parapsychology.

15

must be experienced to be fully appreciated.

What happens to people who are seduced by personal psychic experiences varies. Often they marvel at their own apparent powers, asking themselves, "Do I really have the power to see into the future?" or "Did my touch really make that sick person well?" Some keep this knowledge secret, some are a bit afraid of it, some dissociate themselves from their psychic gifts ("I am just a vessel for this power; don't thank me, thank the power"), and some go wild with fantasies of superhuman strengths.

Scientists researching in the field of psi know they have to help their psychically talented subjects understand the limitations of their psi abilities. But sometimes they forget to warn themselves, and tumble merrily down the hill of subjectivity, leaving behind their erstwhile concerns for objectivity, rigid controls, and the scientific method.

There is an old story of a man who suffered from hallucinations that convinced him he was covered with small, black, crawling bugs. His friends took him to a psychiatrist, and when he had finished describing the imaginary bugs in vivid detail, the psychiatrist brushed off his own arms and snapped, "Well, for heaven's sake, don't let them rub off on me!" In somewhat the same way, psi seems to rub off on some researchers studying it, seducing them into becoming experiencers rather than experimenters. They turn into ideological exponents of psychic powers, draw premature conclusions based on their subjective experiences, and can be found on lecture platforms setting forth unproven theories about psi.

The range of subjective response to possible psi occurrence is as phenomenal as the phenomena. Some who claim to have had psi experiences say they are exhilarating, expanding, different. Others compare them to experiencing new dimensions. And still others find them frightening. Only another lover can understand the compulsion to lay the world at the feet of one's beloved. So, too, only those who believe they have had a meaningful psi experience can understand the resulting compulsion to explain all of psi in terms of one's own personal exposure to it.

So it appears that psi possesses godlike attributes, occult and fraudulent associations, and properties that call forth emotional reactions of excitement and fear. Psi is a phenomenon whose functioning is a mystery, and it exercises a seductive power over many who come into contact with it. All of these factors conspire to cloud the objectivity of all but the most cautious.

II.
Psi

The subject of psi is suffused with mystery, confusion, and ambiguity. Yet, although few are aware of it, laboratory research has yielded a surprising number of facts about the phenomena.

Whether or not the fundamental nature of psi will eventually be resolved as a result of experimental study in the laboratory, researchers have identified some important guideposts. Precise information, vital to anyone attempting to understand a highly complex subject, is now available about psi as a result of research efforts.

The laboratory, then, is the place to begin.

3.
Inside
Laboratory Walls

How can one capture something that is invisible? That appears to have no physical properties whatsoever? That is seemingly without substance, sound waves, magnetism, height, weight, or depth? How can complex monitoring equipment and rigid laboratory procedures be used effectively in pursuit of psi?

Each psi experiment is different, but they all have four basic elements in common. Two of these elements are the *experimenter*, who directs and manages the actual testing, and the *subject*, the person whose potential psi ability is being tested. A third element is the *target*, which consists of either some concealed information to be guessed (There is a painting on the wall in the next room—what is it about?) or an object or event to be affected (We are going to throw a pair of dice ten times—try to make large numbers come up as often as possible.). The last element is the *barrier*, which is one or more shields put between the subject and the target to make sure that whatever happens is due to psi and not to ordinary physical means. The barrier may be great distance separating the subject and the target, a thick cement wall, or just an opaque envelope. Some experiments have additional features but these four are common to all.

Perhaps the easiest way to understand how all this works is to follow the course of one trial of one experiment through the eyes of one of the principals: the subject. What follows is a true story, fully documented, which took place under carefully controlled laboratory conditions and which was observed and recorded by a number of objective witnesses.*

A Psi Hit
The subject of this experiment was Ellen Messer, a twenty-eight-year-old psychiatric nurse at Roosevelt Hospital in Manhattan. Her involvement with psychic research began when she heard a friend's glowing accounts of a course on psychic occurrences and their investigation by scientists.

Messer was intrigued. Ever since she could remember, she had noticed strange coincidences in her life. Nothing dramatic, just little things. She would think of her friend Margaret, and just at that moment Margaret would telephone her. Or in some unlikely, crowded place she would suddenly come face-to-face with a

---

*There are a number of experiments that appear to offer strong and replicable evidence of psi. This particular experiment has been singled out as an example of how an experiment works because it can be easily visualized.

Ellen Messer, who served as a subject in a study using the Ganzfeld technique. Photo by George R. Clovie, New York City.

seemingly aimless; in a word, random. Then if a subject consistently interacts with the target, experimenters may justifiably attribute this success to the presence of psi.

Rigor in both design and execution are precautions to ensure the integrity of experimental results. Experimenters must guard against deception, whereby either inadvertently or through collusion the subject gains access to the target information. They also guard against errors in recording the results. And finally, experimenters must make sure they report their failures as well as their successes.

Replication is a standard scientific precaution against erroneous interpretation or fraud on the part of an experimenter. Scientists publish experimental procedures and results, inviting other, impartial researchers to try the same experiment. They hope the experiment will be repeated and will yield the same positive results for others, indicating that the information gained is indeed reliable.

However, investigators of psi, like psychologists, have found that nothing remains exactly the same where human behavior is involved. As Robert H. Thouless, a former president of Britain's Society for Psychical Research, says, "One can specify the conditions in which one has oneself obtained a successful ESP result without any strong conviction that everyone else who tries will get the same result."[6] Despite this characteristic of all experiments involving human behavior, many physical scientists say they will not admit parapsychology as a science until its experiments are completely repeatable. This may never be possible.

person she had been trying unsuccessfully to call all week.

When she heard that scientists were investigating people's psychic ability, Messer asked around to see if she could find someone doing active research in the New York area. Eventually she heard of a man named Honorton at the Maimonides Medical Center in Brooklyn. She went to see him and volunteered her services.

Charles Honorton, an intense, short man with deep-set eyes, is one of the United States' leading researchers in parapsychology, and has published numerous papers on the subject in specialized professional journals. As Director of Research of the Maimonides Division of Parapsychology and Psychophysics since 1973, Honorton has, with the help of one paid assistant and many volunteers, designed and conducted a number of laboratory experiments to probe psychic phenomena.

Shortly after Messer volunteered for some of the studies in progress, the Honorton group designed a new experimental procedure. They wanted to see whether it was possible to enhance someone's—anyone's—ability to receive psi information by isolating that person from external visual and auditory sensory distractions. A pilot study made by Honorton showed that the procedure (known as the *Ganzfeld technique*) was simple, quick, and startlingly successful.

The Honorton group decided to run a full-scale test using this procedure. Casual visitors to Maimonides were asked if they would like to be tested. Thirty people were used as subjects, and the overall results of the experiment showed that Honorton's approach was indeed effective. The results of these tests were reported by Honorton and his associate Sharon Harper at a parapsychology convention in 1973.[1]

A producer for the National Film Board of Canada heard of Honorton's success and asked permission to film the group in action. The Honorton team agreed, insisting, however, that the camera crew film a real test of their experiment rather than a simulated one. This meant that no one knew for sure whether or not on this particular trial they would be able to successfully achieve psi communication.

Honorton asked Ellen Messer to serve as the subject, and one midafternoon in January 1974, Messer rode the IND subway to Brooklyn. There she joined the experimenters and the film crew in Honorton's eight-room Maimonides Medical Center laboratory.

Honorton explained to the TV crew that Messer would try to receive information being sent to her through psi alone. To do this, she would relax in a leather lounge chair in a soundproof room. Specially designed translucent covers made of split ping-pong balls trimmed with cotton would be placed over her eyes, allowing her to see only a dim red haze. She would be given earphones connected to a recording of soothing, uniform sounds. She would be left entirely alone. For thirty-five minutes she would describe over a microphone all images, thoughts, and feelings passing through her mind. Meanwhile, from a spot three rooms down the hall, completely isolated from Messer, co-experimenter Sharon Harper would try to send her a message via

Subject Ellen Messer in Ganzfeld (a state of
partial sensory deprivation) at Maimonides.
Photo by George R. Clovie, New York City.

psi. If the experiment were successful, Messer would pick up that message while she was in her relaxed state.

When Honorton finished his explanation, everyone's attention turned to Messer. It was time for the experiment to begin. Messer hadn't eaten all day. Just before she went into the soundproof room, she ate two handfuls of M&M candies, a private ritual she had evolved to bring her mental energy to a peak. As a nurse, she did not think there was any significant physiological benefit to the ritual, but she did it anyway; it comforted her.

She leaned back in the reclining chair. For a long time she saw the film crew's bright lights through the ping-pong halves over her eyes. Finally, they finished filming her and went out of the room. For the first time that day, Messer was alone. She relaxed and began describing her thoughts into the waiting microphone.

Now only one person could hear what Messer was saying—Jim Terry, who was recording what she said in a monitoring room next to her soundproof one. At the same time another experimenter in a room down the hall stood in front of a stack of thirty-one identical envelopes and chose one at random. He gave that envelope to Harper.

Harper opened the envelope. Inside were four GAF View-Master slide wheels, each on a different subject. She took the top wheel from the packet and spent five minutes staring intently through a viewer at the seven transparencies on the wheel, trying by psi alone to tell Messer the subject of the wheel which had been chosen. After five minutes she stopped looking at the wheel and settled down to wait until someone would come in to tell her Messer was finished.

In the privacy of her soundproof room, Messer had no way of knowing when Harper started looking at the wheel and when she stopped. She was simply describing the images passing through her mind. Her nervousness was gone; she was relaxed and enjoying herself. Among her early images were women dancing in nightclubs and cowboys in big hats.

After a while, Messer's images changed. According to the tape, she said: "I'm floating over some kind of a landscape. It's surrealistic. Watergate came to my mind. . . . It's the name of a nightclub on 72nd Street (in Manhattan). And marquees— nightclub marquees. Just seeing them. Nightclub marquees . . . in Las Vegas."

Messer went on to describe other images until thirty-five minutes had passed. Then she was handed duplicates of the four different View-Master slide wheels, one of which Harper had been looking at. Which one did Messer think Harper had been trying to send her?

Messer looked through the wheels. No, not this one. No. Then she stopped, and began to shout, "I can't believe it! I just can't believe it!" In her hand she clutched the wheel she knew Harper had been looking at. It was a series of seven photographs of buildings and nightclubs. Buildings and nightclubs in Las Vegas.

Now, several years later, Ellen Messer recalls this experience with mixed emotions. From time to time she continues to participate in experiments at Maimonides, and she has had

Statistical Significance in Psi Tests

ESP (Zener) cards contain pictures of five symbols (star, circle, cross, square, and wavy lines). A deck consists of twenty-five cards, five of each symbol. After a subject has guessed each of the twenty-five cards, he or she has completed a *run*. By chance alone, one would expect five correct correspondences or *hits* in one run.

PK results are evaluated in a similar way. If a die is rolled twenty-four times, any particular number will be expected to appear on the upper face one sixth of the time. By chance alone, one would expect four correct hits out of twenty-four attempts.

To indicate whether psi is operating, statistics are used to evaluate if the number of hits exceeds what would be expected by chance alone. If there is only one possibility in twenty that a given number of hits would have occurred by chance, the experimental results are labeled as statistically significant.

Below is a chart that shows how many hits are needed to achieve statistical significance at the 1 in 20 level, using ESP cards. The more runs done, the closer the average run score can be to chance expectation (five hits in twenty-five trials) and still be statistically significant.

Number of Runs	Number of Trials	Expected Chance Score	Score Needed for Statistical Significance
1		5	9
2		10	16
3		15	22
4		20	28
5		25	34
10		50	63
20	500	100	118
50	1,250	250	278
100	2,500	500	540

several other laboratory successes as spectacular as this one. But this was her first. She says:

Charles Honorton of Maimonides Medical Center in Brooklyn, New York, who adapted the Ganzfeld technique as a tool for psi research.

The general public feels that only specially gifted people can do this, but that's not true at all.

Doing these experiments is fun. It's relaxing to lie down with ping-pong balls over my eyes, letting dreamlike imagery go by. I like watching the pictures, and describing them, and having the feeling that other people are excited by what's going on in my mind.

It's something that I do that has importance. It's possibly giving people information. It's also a task that can be accomplished—that I can accomplish. I know that there are other people who can do it. Anyone who practices can do it. But right now I seem to be able to do this experiment better than many other people.

With Las Vegas, the imagery was so specific and so direct and so just exactly what was on the slide that it was really a mind-blowing experience.

It makes me feel a little bit paranoid, too. I believe in what I'm doing, and I know it works for other people, but it's really amazing that it works for me . . . that I can do it myself, and it works. Just amazing.[2]

Psi vs. Coincidence

Even the best experiment yields evidence of psi only some of the time. Further, in any single test simple coincidence cannot be discounted. For example, Ellen Messer might have been thinking about Las Vegas not because of psi but because of some billboard she had happened to pass on the way to the Maimonides laboratory. Most people have experienced occasional startling coincidences. Since psi apparently has no physical properties, does not operate with a low humming noise, and leaves no tiny footprints on the wall, how can one distinguish between coincidence and psi?

Psi experimenters rely on the mathematical theory of probability to make this crucial distinction. Statistical tables have been developed to evaluate when a series of events falls within the realm of simple chance and when it does not. When the observed events deviate widely and consistently from chance expectation, some factor may be presumed to be causing this deviation. Since a proper psi experiment will have eliminated all other factors, the researcher may be justified in thinking the factor responsible for this deviation from chance is psi.

For example, if subjects attempt to guess whether a coin will land heads or tails, they are expected to be right by chance about 50 percent of the time. That is, if they try one hundred guesses, without psi, they should be correct about fifty times. If they guessed several hundred times, they should still average about fifty correct guesses per one hundred flips.

However, if subjects are able to get sixty-one or more guesses correct out of a hundred, that is beyond what would be expected by chance—in fact, so far beyond that it would happen only one time by chance in 100 trials. In other words, the odds are 100 to 1 against that result.

Chance

One thing experimenters must be sure of is that successful experimental results are not just due to chance. Fortunately a mathematical standard has been devised, based on the mathematical theory of probability, which makes it possible to measure when an event occurs consistently beyond what would be expected by chance alone. The European theorists Geronimo Cardano, Blaise Pascal, and J. Bernouilli first developed this mathematical theory of probability over three hundred years ago. Since then its validity has not been seriously questioned. It has long been used by the physical, biological, and social sciences as a kind of yardstick to evaluate the results of scientific inquiry. For example, in all of psychology, what are considered to be facts have only statistics to justify them.

Initially, statistics' use as a tool for psychical investigations was challenged by some critics, as will soon be described. But in 1937 the Institute of Mathematical Statistics, which is considered the decisive authority on statistical matters in the United States, ruled that it was a completely valid means to evaluate the presence or absence of psi.[3]

The connection between chance and psi is hard for many nonstatisticians to understand. Why can't experimenters simply say, "Psi was here" or "Psi was not here"—why do they instead evaluate its presence or absence numerically?

The answer comes from the elusive nature of psi. It has not yet been possible to create an experiment that elicits significant evidence of psi every single time it is run. Statistical tables permit researchers to describe psi's probable presence or absence numerically. This method can yield some impressive numbers. For example, Honorton estimates that the combined Ganzfeld series done at Maimonides and ten other laboratories gives positive results of 100 billion to 1 over chance.[4] This means that there would be only 1 chance in 100 billion of the experimenters' getting similar results by chance.

Overall, psi experimentation follows the same order as that followed by other scientific experiments. The experimenter thinks up an idea about the subject under investigation, tests its validity through experimentation, and publishes the results. If a number of other independent scientists obtain similar results, the original idea is believed confirmed, and is added to the sum total of human knowledge—unless, of course, yet another scientist can come up with a different idea and prove that it makes nonsense out of the first one. As the medical writer Michael Crichton, M.D., puts it:

Strictly speaking, no hypothesis or theory can ever be proven. It can only be disproven. When we say we believe a theory, what we really mean is that we are unable to show that the theory is wrong—not that we are able to show, beyond doubt, that the theory is right.

A scientific theory may stand for years, even centuries, and it may accumulate hundreds of bits of corroborating evidence to support it. Yet a theory is always vulnerable, and a single conflict-

ing finding is all that is required to throw the hypothesis into disarray, and call for a new theory. One can never know when such conflicting evidence will arise. Perhaps it will happen tomorrow, perhaps never. But the history of science is strewn with the ruins of mighty edifices toppled by an accident, or a triviality.[5]

New theories, then, topple old ones standing in their path. One such theory, possessing enormous toppling power, is that psi exists. The next chapter examines the evidence advanced in support of that controversial theory.

How the Ganzfeld procedure works: (Left) A sender concentrates on a View Master slide. (Middle) The subject describes images he receives in Ganzfeld. (Right) The subject attempts to choose the slide the sender concentrated on.

When experiments yield successful results of 1,000 to 1 over chance, or even more, the figures mean that there are very high odds against the result being due to accident or statistical chance. Researchers then assume that there was some kind of psi operating to get the correct answers.

4.
Psi Exists

Researchers currently engaged in the active investigation of psi base their assertion that psi's existence has been scientifically demonstrated on the considerable laboratory evidence amassed to date. When they evaluated this question for the museum exhibit, the Psi SEARCH advisors* estimated that some six hundred accounts of psi experiments published in recognized professional journals give significant evidence of psi.[1] Dr. Charles T. Tart, Professor of Psychology at the University of California at Davis, says, "As far as I'm concerned, the people who don't believe or won't believe in it are the people who just haven't really read the old evidence."[1]

Many scientists disagree, aligning themselves firmly with the famous German physicist Herman von Helmholtz (1821–1894), who asserted, "Neither the testimony of all the Fellows of the Royal Society, nor even the evidence of my own senses, would lead me to believe in the transmission of thought from one person to another independently of the recognized channels of sense."[3] D. O. Hebb, Professor of Psychology at McGill University in Canada, states, "Personally, I do not accept ESP for a moment, because it does not make sense."[4] Another distinguished psychologist, C. E. M. Hansel of the University of Wales, and perhaps the field's most diligent critic, wrote in 1966, "A great deal of time, effort, and money has been expended but an acceptable demonstration of the existence of extrasensory perception has not been given." [5]

Nonetheless, most psi researchers feel psi's existence is no longer in question. As K. Ramakrishna Rao, Professor of Psychology at Andhra University, India, puts it, "The scientist who is, at this stage, averse to accepting the evidence for ESP reminds me of the dogmatic professors of philosophy who refused to look through Galileo's telescope."[6]

The evidence to which Rao refers comes from hundreds of tests of psi conducted by numerous scientists over the last half century. Perhaps best known is the extraordinary research team of Dr. Louisa E. Rhine and Dr. J. B. Rhine. And for good reason. Over a lifetime of work, much of it done at North Carolina's Duke University, the Rhines have methodically piled up extensive evidence that psi exists. Others have added significantly to the evidence,

*Dr. Robert Morris of the University of California at Santa Barbara, Dr. Robert Van de Castle of the University of Virginia, and Dr. Stanley Krippner of the Humanistic Psychology Institute, San Francisco.

One of the earliest laboratories where the investigation of psychic phenomena took place. The experimenter is H. Price.

but the Rhines' systematic experiments over a period of fifty years offered the first substantial, scientific proof of psi's existence.

Today, nearly half a century after J. B. Rhine's first major publication,[7] many people automatically think of the Rhines and the Duke Laboratory when the subject of parapsychology comes up. This public awareness reflects the influence of that work and the publicity it received. Much of that publicity was extremely unfavorable. Even now the controversy that arose with the publication of their various psi experiments continues to color many people's attitude toward psi.

The Duke work focused on two major questions about human psychic abilities. The first was whether people can somehow discover concealed information without the use of the senses. The second question was whether people can somehow influence external events by other than ordinary means. In both cases the results of the Rhines' experiments yielded a resounding "yes, people can."

In order to understand laboratory research into psi, one must cope with four rather cumbersome terms. These terms—*telepathy, clairvoyance, precognition,* and *psychokinesis*—refer to four aspects of psi. The Rhines initiated a policy of focusing research on these four cornerstones, and they remain the focus of research efforts today. These are the only aspects of psi that most

Louisa E. and J. B. Rhine, pioneers in the scientific investigation of psi.

psi researchers will agree have been demonstrated in the laboratory.

Three of these terms refer to ways people can get information without the help of the five senses. The first way, telepathy, is to perceive the thoughts of another person. The second way, clairvoyance, is to perceive the information directly, somewhat like using x-ray vision to see through a thick wall. The third way, precognition, is to perceive information about future events before they happen.

Psychokinesis, the fourth cornerstone, differs sharply from the other three. While they are concerned with the receiving of information, psychokinesis—or PK, as it is usually called—is concerned with sending information out. Specifically, PK refers to influence somehow being exerted on the environment by mental processes alone. The word is taken from the Greek words for mind and motion, and PK is often popularly referred to as mind over matter.

ESP, PK, and the Rhines

In their early work the researchers at Duke went to a great deal of trouble to try to distinguish the first three supposed psi abilities from one another and so to identify exactly which one was used by a subject at any particular time. After further work, however, the Duke researchers eventually abandoned this practice. They felt that it was nearly impossible to identify whether a subject was using telepathy, clairvoyance, or precognition at any particular time.

Imagine, for instance, that a researcher hid a coin under a pillow and then asked a subject to guess what was hidden there. Supposing that the experimental conditions were such that the subject could know the answer only by means of psi, how can the researcher determine to which subcategory the subject's correct response of "a coin" belongs? Did the subject read the researcher's mind to find the answer, and so rely on telepathy, or simply "see" what was under the pillow through clairvoyance? Or perhaps the subject dreamt of a coin the night before, in a precognitive dream. Subjects often get the correct answer to the question posed by a psi experiment, but rarely know how they got that answer.

Therefore, J. B. Rhine joined telepathy, clairvoyance, and precognition together under the general name of *extrasensory perception* (ESP), a term he invented. This practice is followed in this book. Nevertheless, researchers still assert that the existence of each separate phenomenon has been demonstrated in the laboratory (with the possible exception of pure telepathy), and the four terms are still much in use.

The results of the experimental ESP series done at Duke University in 1929 were reported by J. B. Rhine in 1934. Rhine interpreted the results as indicating the occurrence of ESP.[9] In a total of 85,724 experimental trials run over a period of five years, subjects were asked to identify concealed test cards. Subjects were able to do so with odds that were better than 100 to 1 (sometimes astronomically better than 100 to 1) against chance. These results were accepted by statisticians as significant, indicating the presence of some factor other than chance.

During the experiment, they ran one series of 1,850 trials with results over chance of 10^{22} to 1 (10^{22} equals 10,000,000,000,000,000,000,000—a number so big that even in these inflationary times there is no word in common usage to name it). The experimental controls used for this series—known as the Pearce–Pratt series—are today considered tight by most researchers,[10] although at least one critic, C. E. M. Hansel, strongly disagrees.[11] In the experiment the Rhines asked the subject, Pearce, to identify the order of cards in a pack handled by the sender, Pratt. Pearce and Pratt were kept in separate buildings, and precautions were taken to prevent communication by means other than psi. The extraordinary results of the Pearce–Pratt series remain among the most convincing experimental results of psi experiments yet obtained under controlled laboratory conditions.

J. B. Rhine first reported this material in a publication entitled *Extra-Sensory Perception*.[12] Confirming reports by other researchers soon began to appear, showing that, both at Duke and elsewhere, ESP was being taken seriously. This sparked a controversy over the validity of the ESP findings.

Louisa E. Rhine and J. B. Rhine

The Rhines, who were childhood neighbors, attended Wooster College in Ohio in 1917. There Louisa Rhine majored in botany. J. B. Rhine began as a preministerial student, but, he says, "I gave it up when I found in psychology that there was no accepted scientific basis for the existence of the will. Without free will the ministry seemed futile."[8] After World War I, the Rhines married and moved to Chicago in 1920. When they obtained their Ph.D.'s in plant physiology from the University of Chicago, they moved again, this time to Cambridge, Massachusetts. There they went to Harvard, hoping to study what was at the time called "psychical research" under Professor William McDougall, then a staff member of that university's psychology department. Not long after, McDougall went to Duke University, and with his approval the Rhines followed in 1927. There, under McDougall's directorship, Rhine founded the Duke Parapsychology Laboratory, and the Rhines began what became their life work examining the existence and nature of psi.

Standard ESP (Zener) cards, showing the
five neutral symbols used as targets.

An early experimental trial underway at
Duke University using ESP (Zener) cards.

30

The Controversy

In the six years following the original Rhine publication, almost sixty critical articles by forty different authors appeared in the professional literature. The criticism, as analyzed by Charles Honorton in a 1975 article called "Error Some Place!"[13] fell into two major categories. The first revolved around the experimental procedures used. Did the experimenters unwittingly or intentionally give their subjects sensory clues as to the correct response? Did the Rhines' practice of hand-shuffling the cards (abandoned in later work) distort the results? The second type of criticism focused on the mathematics used to evaluate the results. Was the Rhines' estimate of what could be expected by chance correct? Had they used the proper statistical procedure to analyze their results? Were their results simply caused by quirks in probability theory? All of these criticisms were refuted.

From 1937 on, the *Journal of Parapsychology* carried additional studies done in the Duke Laboratory and elsewhere that dispelled much of the criticism of their experimental procedures. That same year the Institute of Mathematical Statistics undertook to rule on the validity of using the statistics of probability as a measure of psi. The president of the institute released the following statement for publication:

> Dr. Rhine's investigations have two aspects: experimental and statistical. On the experimental side mathematicians of course have nothing to say. On the statistical side, however, recent mathematical work has established the fact that, assuming that the experiments have been properly performed, the statistical analysis is essentially valid. If the Rhine investigation is to be fairly attacked, it must be on other than mathematical grounds.[14]

By 1940 thirty-three experiments involving nearly one million experimental trials under carefully controlled conditions were published by a number of experimenters, including the staff at the Duke Laboratory. Twenty-seven of the thirty-three experiments yielded statistically significant results.[15] Nonetheless, many critics declined to accept the evidence as valid, even after their specific criticisms had been answered.

The Rhines and others persisted. In March 1943 the *Journal of Parapsychology* published a summary of nine years of testing the fourth cornerstone of psi: PK. This work yielded positive results at odds of 1 trillion to 1 over chance.

While their earlier work had dealt with ESP, using concealed cards, this work focused on PK, using dice. It tested subjects' abilities to influence mentally the fall of dice as they were thrown. Using the power of their minds alone, subjects were asked sometimes to make high dice combinations come up (8s or better when two dice were thrown), sometimes low combinations (6s or less, again when two dice were used). At first the dice were tumbled by hand. Later, they were tossed mechanically. They were released over corrugated surfaces down inclined planes so that their fall was totally randomized.

Partly because of the outcry that had greeted their major publication concerning ESP, the Duke researchers held back their PK results.[16] Finally in 1943 they started publishing the accumulated

Testing ESP

For many ESP tests, special cards are used to provide neutral target material. These were developed by J.B. Rhine in consultation with Dr. Karl Zener, an expert in perception. Zener cards consist of pictures of five symbols (star, circle, cross, square, and wavy lines). A deck contains twenty-five cards, five of each symbol.

The Duke Laboratory developed several different testing procedures using these cards. One was to ask the subject to guess the order of the symbols as a sender turned the cards, one at a time, behind an opaque screen or in another room. A second was to guess the order of the cards in a newly shuffled deck before anyone looked at it. Here, too, the cards were screened from the subject's view. A third was to tell a subject that a deck was about to be shuffled, and to ask him to predict the order the cards would take after shuffling. In a fourth procedure, the subject was asked to try to identify the card order of a well-shuffled deck simply placed in a box on the table in front of him or her.

After guessing each of the twenty-five cards, the subject had completed a *run*. By chance alone, one would expect five correct correspondences, or *hits, in such a run.*

An early experiment in psychokinesis underway at Duke University. J. B. Rhine is on the left.

findings.[17] Despite the 1 trillion to 1 overall results, the Rhines did not expect overwhelming acceptance because of the many years of controversy surrounding their earlier work. Nor did they gain it. In 1943 the world was in the midst of World War II. Despite considerable press coverage, the new results attracted comparatively little attention until later. The only statistics of general concern at the time were war casualties in Europe, Asia, and Africa.

Negative reaction to this new report, when it came, charged recording errors, fraud, and something called *dice bias*. This last charge referred to the possibility that a flaw might be present in the dice, which would result in some numbers appearing more often than would normally happen by chance. The Duke researchers had pointed out in their original report on PK that subjects were asked sometimes to make high combinations appear and sometimes to make low combinations appear. No flaw in the dice—if indeed one were present—would work well with both high and low numbers.

The Anatomy of an Experiment

Steps Used to Investigate Phenomena	*Special Steps Needed to Test Psi Phenomena*
Define an area of investigation.	
Select some aspect for study.	
Postulate an hypothesis.	
Test the hypothesis.	
a. Ask a question.	
b. Devise a test.	Select an organism presumably capable of psi interaction. This organism becomes the subject for the experiment.
	Select target material (something in the environment) for interaction.
	Design some barrier(s) to block off all communication between the two by any usual sensory means (if the test is for ESP) or motor means (if the test is for PK).
	Establish a line of communication to be followed: either create a message as the target and see how the subject responds (ESP), or require the subject to influence something in a specific way and see if the influence is effective (PK).
c. Describe what happens (note the results).	Assess how precise the information exchange has been between the subject and target. (This may need to be done by some judging procedure.)
d. Summarize the findings.	Determine whether the psi exchange was sufficiently beyond the level of chance to warrant conclusions about psi (significance of results).
e. Check for experimental flaws or alternative explanations.	Psi testing requires extensive precautions to avoid experimental flaws in above steps, and since it relies on statistical practices for measurement, the handling of these must be checked for applicability and accuracy.
Evaluate the hypothesis in terms of the results.	
Optional:	
Suggest possibilities for further research.	
Suggest relationship to general knowedge of how the universe works.	

A further validation of the Rhines' work came some years after the experiments were conducted. Several psi researchers noticed a curious phenomenon in their own work, which they called the *decline effect*. Under the decline effect, subjects start by giving strong evidence of psi, but over repeated testing their rate of psi success declines. The first PK paper from Duke indicated that the subjects had done better near the start of their individual test sessions than they did toward the end. A check of the first run of each subject's record sheet against the last run of the same sheet revealed a consistent and significant difference. When the researchers examined the whole of the PK work for this decline, it was found to be highly significant—at odds of 1 million to 1.

Rhine himself views this discovery as the most satisfactory kind of evidence that psi exists. The decline effect would not be expected to affect results due to recording errors, faulty experimental procedures, or abnormalities in the dice. If any such distorting elements had been present, they would be expected to remain constant. Since the results fluctuated in a way that indicated the presence of the decline effect, only psi remained as the factor responsible for the experimental results.[18]

In 1965 J. B. Rhine retired from Duke University, and the Duke Parapsychology Laboratory was replaced by the Foundation for Research on the Nature of Man, a privately funded research foundation, which Rhine established to continue the work begun at Duke.

The Rhines, now in their eighties, live quietly and unpretentiously on a farm near Durham. Since 1948 Louisa Rhine has specialized in collecting and analyzing cases of possible spontaneous psi occurrences and has written several books. J. B. Rhine remains accessible, easy to meet, and still willing to write and give interviews on the subject of psi's existence. When asked how he feels about continued refusal on the part of many scientists to accept that psi's existence has been demonstrated, J. B. Rhine says, "I realize better now that in parapsychology we are investigating an incomparably difficult field—the extrasensory, extraphysical psi ability—while at the same time the world is being academically educated to rely only upon the *sensate* physical world as real. Psi research, however, is now studying the underlying unity of these conflicting orders of reality to discover how best to interpret their relation."[19]

The Rhines' leadership, even dominance of the field of psi, was long unchallenged, and the stamp of their personalities is even now clearly evident. Almost every major researcher in the field was trained by them or at least did some work in their lab. The Rhines' basic theory about psi was strongly impressed on these researchers. It is that psi is to be found, to a greater or lesser extent, in nearly every individual, and that it is totally different from anything else. Their belief that psi is probably universal won it many friends among the public. On the other hand, they are also convinced that psi is nonphysical. Their insistence that psi is fundamentally different from everything that can be detected by the five senses made psi virtually an orphan by discouraging scientists belonging to other disciplines from taking an interest in the field.

The Random Number Generator

Along with the Rhines, many other researchers find evidence of psi. An important contribution was made by the German physicist Helmut Schmidt, who came to their lab in 1969. Schmidt became intrigued with psi for the same reason that many other scientists reject it: "Because psi does not fit into the system."[20] According to his traditional physics training, psi simply could not exist. Schmidt decided to find out for himself if it did.

Schmidt's efforts revolve around a machine he constructed called a random number generator (RNG). The Boeing Company had given permission for him to do some of the development work on the project while he was in their employ. His RNG work brought mechanized methods to the Rhines' classic dice-tossing test, and the results he obtained exceeded what would be expected by chance by odds of over 10,000 to 1.[21] Furthermore, other researchers have been able to obtain evidence of psi with the RNG.[22]

Schmidt's RNG device enables successful subjects to provide an intriguing demonstration of mind over matter. Many different subjects, in many different experimental trials, have shown themselves apparently able to "will" lights in a ring on top of the RNG to move clockwise or counterclockwise. The machine provides an automatic source of random numbers that researchers consider at least as reliable statistically as tossing dice. It generates these numbers much faster than the old dice-tossing procedure, which required rolling the dice, recording the results, picking the dice up, rolling them again, and so on. Schmidt asked subjects to try to influence the numbers generated by the machine in the same way that the Rhines' subjects had tried to influence the numbers generated by throwing dice: that is, to make the numbers consistently higher or consistently lower than would occur by chance alone. Many different subjects have been able to do this.

In addition to providing significant evidence of the existence of psi, results obtained with Schmidt's machine indicate that humans may not need to consciously understand the exact nature of physical events in order to interact with them. By successfully influencing the machine, the subjects apparently did something with their minds that, had they been allowed to take the machine apart and play with it, they probably would not have been able to do with their hands.

Schmidt's work also has helped to eliminate the claim by skeptics that the positive evidence of PK obtained from dice and coin-tossing experiments would disappear with a larger sample. Some critics believed the results obtained by the Rhines and others could have been due to simple coincidence. The RNG machine, which made it possible for researchers to run an enormous number of PK trials, effectively disproved that charge.

Today Schmidt is a research associate at the Mind Science Foundation in San Antonio, Texas, where he continues to study the mysteries of psi. He believes that the search for psi is a search for a new law of nature, and that when that law is discovered, it will prove to be some principle physicists have heretofore overlooked.[23]

What the RNG does to strengthen evidence of the existence of

How a Random Number Generator Works

A random number generator (RNG) provides researchers with a useful tool to test psi ability. The name random number generator is somewhat misleading, because the machine does not generate numbers. Instead, it provides a source of random events. Subjects are asked to attempt to impose an order on these random events through pk.

Several different types of RNGs exist today. One type, the first invented by Helmut Schmidt, relies on a radioactive substance called Strontium 90. It is a natural property of Strontium 90 that its subatomic particles are constantly deteriorating in a random fashion. The RNGs rectangular metal box contains a small amount of Strontium 90 and a device somewhat like a Geiger counter that monitors the arrival time of particles emitted by the Strontium 90 as it decays. Also present in the box is an electronic counter that is rapidly counting 1,2,1,2,1,2 over and over, thousands of times a second. The exact arrival time of each particle emitted by the decaying Strontium 90 is used to generate an electrical signal that stops the counter at either the 1 or the 2 position. When not subject to psi influence, particles stop the counter randomly, sometimes at the 1 position, sometimes at the 2 position. Subjects are essentially asked to stop the counter as consistently as possible in one of the two positions.

But subjects are not asked to think about influencing subatomic particles. Instead, the machine is designed so that each time the counter stops, its position is indicated through a circle of small light bulbs (see illustration). When the machine is turned on, one of these bulbs lights up. After that, every time the counter stops on 2, the light moves to the next bulb in a clockwise direction. When it stops on 1, the light moves to the next bulb in a counterclockwise direction.

A random number generator. Note the circle of light bulbs.

Subjects are asked sometimes to will the light to move clockwise and sometimes to will the light to move counterclockwise. A digital read-out displays the total number of movements of the light in the direction requested by the experimenter. The light moves a total of 100 times in each run, accomplished over a period of a few minutes.

Most subjects are not aware that the movement of the lights reflects the effect of subatomic particles on an electronic counter. Even when so informed, few could be expected to understand exactly how such a process worked. Nonetheless, subjects do significantly alter the movement of the lights. Scientists do not yet know how they manage to do this. They may do so by directly altering the rate of deterioration of Strontium 90 or by affecting the counter, or they may somehow bypass that whole process and simply influence the lights directly.

The machine provides an automatic source of randomness that researchers consider mathematically and scientifically reliable. This is because the counter inside the RNG, when uninfluenced, registers a roughly equal number of 1s and 2s, an indication that it is behaving randomly. It is sometimes left running between tests and checked to be sure that its behavior is still random.

PK, the Ganzfeld technique introduced by Charles Honorton at Maimonides is doing for ESP. One trial of this experiment involving Ellen Messer was discussed in the previous chapter. The Ganzfeld procedure has been successfully repeated by William Braud and Lendell Braud at the University of Houston,[24] Michael York at the University of California at Santa Barbara,[25] and Rex Stanford at St. John's University,[26] to name a few. Some researchers have also been unsuccessful at times with the Ganzfeld procedure. According to Honorton's count, out of 26 separate studies 14 produced significant psi results. Honorton believes this makes 100 billion to 1 odds a "conservative" overall statement of the Ganzfeld's success.[27]

Rhine's ESP and PK trials, Schmidt's RNG, and Honorton's Ganzfeld work are together considered by many observers to be among the most important experiments to offer evidence in favor of psi's existence. These experimental procedures have been shown to work successfully with a wide variety of people as subjects. The results of each have held up over a long series of trials. And each has been successfully repeated by other researchers, providing a dependable means of obtaining evidence of psi.

Results with a Sensitive

Irrespective of the technique used, strong evidence of psi is frequently best obtained through the testing of sensitives, popularly known as psychics. These are people from all walks of life who, for reasons no one yet knows, appear to have exceptional psi ability. Thousands of self-professed sensitives can be found, but only a few have been able to demonstrate superior psi ability under rigorously controlled laboratory conditions.

One such person is Lalsingh Harribance, a thirty-seven-year-old man of East Indian descent raised in Trinidad. Working with William G. Roll, a parapsychologist who is the project director of the Psychical Research Foundation in Durham, North Carolina, Harribance has participated in a number of highly successful experimental series. One of these yielded results superior to chance by odds of 100 trillion to 1—that is, 100,000,000,000,000 to 1.[28] Extraordinary experimental results like these convince researchers who encounter them that there can be no question of psi's existence.

Sensitives are as individualistic as the rest of humanity. Lalsingh Harribance possesses a strong personality, thinly shielded by a quiet, unobtrusive air. Experimenters report that he urges them to devise extremely stringent controls for experiments in which he participates so as to remove the possibility of any alternative explanation for successful results. A convert to Christianity from Hinduism about a decade ago, Harribance is said to think of his psi abilities as spiritual powers.[29]

In the experiment under discussion here, researcher Roll asked Harribance to determine by means of psi alone which of a number of concealed photographs were of men and which were of women. The experiment was run by a co-experimenter of Roll's, a research assistant in the laboratory, named Judith Klein. They used ten photographs, five of females and five of males, pasted on cards. Because only two choices were possible—male or

Helmut Schmidt conducting a PK
experiment using a random number
generator.

Experimenter Judith Klein with the sensitive Lalsingh Harribance.

female—Harribance would be expected to guess correctly 50 percent of the time by chance alone. The experimenters felt successful psi was evidenced by the fact that Harribance was correct far more than half the time.

The experiment worked as follows. Klein would shuffle the cards and then place them face down, without looking at them, on top of a padded table. Harribance stayed in a second room, separated from Klein and the cards by a wall half a foot thick. When signalled that Klein had finished placing the cards on the table, Harribance would mark on a record sheet the order in which he guessed the cards to be, then signal back that he was done. Klein would record the actual order of the cards after Harribance finished guessing. (The signal was not verbal; Harribance either knocked on the wall or pressed a buzzer.)

Harribance made his guesses quickly, almost without thinking, spending about one-half second on each. He did not appear to use conscious deliberation in making his choices, nor did he try to balance his calls evenly between male and female. Every day for ten days Harribance did ten runs of ten cards each for a total of one thousand trials per experimental series.

The first series yielded results at odds of 10,000 to 1 over chance. As Harribance grew more comfortable with the process, the results improved dramatically, up to the 100 trillion to 1 results already mentioned.

In retrospect, Roll views the results of his work with Harribance as by far the most remarkable of his entire professional career as an investigator of psi.[30] Further, he says that he regards Harribance as one of the most outstanding of all the sensitives who have participated in laboratory research. Roll speculates that the remarkable results of this particular experiment may have been due at least in part to two factors in addition to Harribance's innate gifts as a sensitive. The first was that Harribance enjoyed an especially warm and supportive relationship with two members of the experimental team, Judith Klein and John Stump. The second was that Harribance consistently prayed and meditated before the experimental sessions began. Roll thinks that these practices helped Harribance to relax, and that his increased relaxation may have enhanced his performance.[31]

No Easy Answers

Despite all the cumulative evidence of psi offered by these and other experiments, conclusive proof of psi's existence is not generally conceded. Anyone who says "psi's existence has been proven in the laboratory" is likely to be greeted with scornful hoots from a great number of people. Non-psi scientists and academicians, though accustomed to the statistical approach, find that psi blatantly contradicts basic assumptions they hold concerning man and his place in nature. So they refuse to accept the evidence. Other people—especially nonmathematicians—do not understand statistics. Statistics yield the impressive odds of 100 trillion to 1 for one of the Harribance series. Yet what actually happened was that Harribance guessed 677 cards correctly out of 1,000 when 500 correct guesses would be expected by chance, a difference which nonmathematicians tend to dismiss as unimpressive.

K. Ramakrishna Rao, one of the researchers who successfully repeated Rhine's ESP experiments.

Both scientists and nonscientists alike find it disconcerting that not every researcher who tries to repeat one of the leading psi experiments can do so successfully. Psi critic Hansel lists *unsuccessful* attempts to repeat Rhine's ESP experiments by other researchers at Colgate University, Southern Methodist University, Brown University, and Johns Hopkins University.[32] If the experiments can be repeated successfully by some people (as they were by experimenters at the University of Colorado, Columbia University, Hunter College, and Harvard University, among others), why can't they be repeated successfully by everyone? Rao offers this explanation: "The experimenter's personality, his attitudes towards psi in general and the subject in particular, his mannerisms, his mood, his enthusiasm, his perceptiveness, the clarity with which he presents his test, the confidence he instills into his subject, and a host of other factors are likely to make up the psychological complex that accounts for his success or failure."[33] This *experimenter effect,* as it has been called, suggests that there may be a strong connection between the experimenter and his or her own experimental results.

Margaret Mead says that in psi experiments "tremendous efforts have been used which far outstrip the normal procedures to guarantee scientific credibility. . . . We may well ask why it is necessary, in studies of this kind, to have at least twice as many

William G. Roll of the Psychical Research Foundation who tested Lalsingh Harribance.

safeguards and artificial substitutes for integrity as those usually demanded."[34] Perhaps the answer is the third major reason that psi's existence still stirs up such a controversy. That is, because it runs contrary to what most people view as established laws of nature. As Gardner Murphy has written, only a deep belief in these laws would inspire scientists to accuse psi researchers ". . . of rampant and egregious fraud."[35]

Nonetheless, the results of the experiments by Rhine, Schmidt, Honorton, Roll, and others convince most psi researchers beyond any reasonable doubt that psi does exist. Indeed, some would say that one of the most amazing aspects of the whole history of scientific research into the subject is not that psi exists. Rather it is that much of the public remains unaware of how firmly most researchers in the field agree that psi's existence has been proven. In accordance with that consensus, most experiments testing psi today presuppose its existence. They focus on particular aspects of the phenomenon, hoping that from knowledge of the particular will come the answer to the fundamental and still unsolved mystery of exactly how psi interaction occurs.

Although the core problem of how psi works remains unresolved, useful answers are emerging from the research. Scientists now believe they are able to supply some interesting observations in response to four key questions: Who can successfully use psi? What can be communicated by psi? When does psi occur? Where must one be in order for psi to occur? These questions and the theories associated with them will be discussed in the chapters that follow.

5.
Who Can Use Psi?

Who can use psi? Perhaps most people.

Psi may be a nearly universal ability. As Gardner Murphy puts it, "We are concerned with generic and not simply with individual gifts."[1] Psi researcher Charles Tart says, "We do believe that everyone may well have been born with ESP talent . . ."[2]

Tests indicate that people do differ as to how much use they can make of psi. Laboratory study appears to confirm the general notion that some people—sensitives—have exceptional psi ability. Tart calls these people "superstars."[3] But laboratory tests also indicate that psi may be generally distributed in the population, irrespective of age, sex, or intelligence.[4] Basing their opinion on the collective evidence of several hundred experiments showing successful psi in randomly chosen groups of subjects, the Psi SEARCH exhibition advisors agreed that, "Everyone seems to have potential psi ability."[5]

Psi in the General Public

Many successful experimental results have been obtained using ordinary people exclusively. The groups tested by Rhine, Schmidt, Honorton, and others were virtually unscreened. Honorton describes the subjects of his first Ganzfeld series as "mostly casual visitors to the lab."[6] Rhine described the twenty-five subjects of an early experiment as "our colleagues of the Parapsychological Laboratory and of the Department of Psychology, a few graduate students, two of our children, then aged 5 and 7 years, and ourselves."[7] If they were ready to be tested, Rhine was ready to test them. As he wrote, "There was no selection of subject except on the basis of interest. If one was eager to try the test, he was eligible."[8]

Experimental evidence published to date indicates that factors such as age, sex, and intelligence do not appear to significantly affect psi ability. Several experimenters have tested the relationship of I.Q. to psi ability. One, Dr. Robert Brier, of Long Island University, found that people with extremely high I.Q.s gave strong negative evidence of psi.[9] Some, such as Betty Humphrey, who worked with J. B. Rhine, found a very slight positive relationship; others have found essentially none.[10] Most investigators would agree with Michael Scriven, Professor of Philosophy at the University of California at Berkeley, that "there is no strong evidence at the present moment for a correlation between extrasensory capacity and intelligence."[11]

Clearly, no definitive answers have yet been found. All that is known so far is that many men, women, and children of different ages and of different intellectual backgrounds have had significant successes with the Rhines' experiments, with Schmidt's RNG, with Honorton's Ganzfeld technique, and with many other psi tests. But scientists have just scratched the surface in this area. Although no distinguishing factors have yet been found, some may be uncovered by future research.

A good deal of research has focused on the question of whether particular personality traits may be related to psi use. Psychology professor Gertrude Schmeidler identified several characteristics common to high-scoring subjects in psi experiments. She found that people who were friendly and outgoing seemed to do better at psi tests.[12] She also found that people were most successful with psi tasks who either believed in or accepted the possibility of psi's existence. A similar correlation has been found by many other researchers.[13] In a different experiment, Charles Honorton found greater psi success among people who had good visual imagery[14] and the ability to recall their dreams.[15] Here too, however, the results remain fragmentary and inconclusive. A profile of the perfect psi subject is apparently still a long way off.

In the course of their experimental work, researchers have discovered some curious effects in connection with psi. One that they consider extremely important is called *psi missing*. Psi missing occurs when a subject shows evidence of negative psi at odds far greater than chance. People who psi miss are consistently wrong in psi guesses—much more frequently than they would be simply by chance. Researchers believe such people may, for some reason, be uncomfortable with the testing situation or may have a deep unconscious need to reject psi information, whether because of their cultural background, skepticism about psi's existence, or other as yet undiscovered factors.[16] Researchers maintain that psi is still operating in these people because they miss so consistently. If psi were not operating in these people, then they would have a greater number of correct answers—approximately as many as would be expected by chance.

Another curious psi effect has already been touched on in the previous chapter. It is the *decline effect*, the phenomenon first encountered by Charles Richet in the 1880s and later by others as well. J. B. Rhine found it in both his ESP and PK tests. Under the decline effect, psi simply dribbles away. Some experiments start out by working well and yielding positive results, and then, as they are repeated and repeated, yield results that are less and less significant, until finally the results simply resemble chance. Sometimes the results even go below chance to the level of psi-missing. No one knows what accounts for the decline effect. Perhaps subjects get bored as experimental trials are run and rerun.

While the decline effect has not yet been explained, several researchers are trying to discover ways to counteract it. One researcher currently doing battle with the decline effect is Charles Tart. He reasoned that if subjects received immediate feedback about the success or failure of their ESP guesses, their results might improve instead of declining. Tart decided to have his subjects work with ten playing cards and try to guess which one a sender was concentrating on in another room. After the subject

Charles Tart of the University of California at Davis, who is trying to counter the decline effect.

made his or her choice, a light came on to indicate the correct answer and, if the guess was correct, a bell rang. Tart reports that the results ranged from odds of flat chance to odds of over a trillion trillion to 1 over chance.[17]

Tart's method of providing immediate feedback does appear to enhance psi performance and thus curtail the decline effect. In addition, it seems to help subjects learn more clearly just how it feels to correctly choose a target via psi. Frequent practice with Tart's technique apparently helps some subjects succeed more often with psi.

About his technique, Tart says,

> Some of the right guesses are bound to be chance-induced, and immediate feedback to a chance-induced hit can't help you learn anything. So in practice immediate feedback doesn't mean that just anybody can learn ESP. We do believe that everyone may well have been born with ESP talent, but, given our cultural conditioning, such talent will have been pretty well repressed. So, by and large, you'd expect feedback to produce no improvement in a person with no discernible talent—just as a blind man can't get better in a color-discrimination test. With some talent—the vast majority of cases—you'd expect feedback to produce a balance between learning and confusion, leading to a steady-state performance—itself a major improvement. And in quite talented and highly motivated percipients the learning process should predominate—the qualification here being that motivation is just as important to learning as natural talent is.[18]

Although scientists such as Tart appear to be making progress in devising techniques that facilitate psi exchange, such work is still in the early stages. Researchers express great concern about the many currently popular commercial courses and programs that claim to enhance psi ability. Such claims are often gravely overstated, they say, and some of the practices can even be harmful to the amateur trying them out. Dr. Rex. G. Stanford, Research Director of the Center for Parapsychological Research in Austin, Texas, maintains that some of the courses that purport to enhance individuals' psi abilities "may not be healthy for persons who already have some serious psychological problem."[19] Researchers agree that no commercial psi training course currently being taught has been adequately tested scientifically, and they urge the public to exercise great care in experimenting with these techniques.

The Specially Gifted

In addition to their work with ordinary people, psi researchers also study sensitives. One major reason for this is that sensitives are more able to demonstrate psi than the ordinary person. As Charles Tart points out, "...they're able to provide a strong, steady flow of ESP."[20] Naturally, experimenters find this steady flow useful in the laboratory.

In addition, sensitives often offer researchers valuable insights into the workings of psi. Aware of their unusual gifts, sensitives have had the opportunity to reflect on how they use psi in their own lives. They are often more conscious of the psi process. Charles Honorton wrote that one of the elements that inspired a

A subject (shown on the television screen) tries to choose which card the sender is concentrating on.

pilot test of his Ganzfeld experiment was "the introspected accounts of 'gifted' subjects."[21] Gertrude Schmeidler, well known for her work both with sensitives and with persons of average psi ability, modified the structure of an experiment based on suggestions from a sensitive subject.[22] She has stated that in her research she has benefited greatly from a sensitive's recommendations as to the proper "care and feeding" of subjects.[23]

Some psi experiments require highly complex monitoring equipment. However, monitoring large groups of subjects can be immensely costly, and most experimenters suffer from a chronic shortage of research funds. Fortunately for researchers struggling with tight budgets, a series of tests with single subjects may yield results equal in statistical importance to tests with large groups of subjects (depending on the nature of the problem being investigated). It is obviously less expensive to monitor just one person than a large and unwieldy group of subjects. A sensitive is nearly always used in such instances.

When psi research was first brought into the laboratory, most researchers generally shunned commercial and popular sensitives because the historical record showed that many of them gave their gifts an extra boost by cheating. Naturally anxious to avoid contaminating their results by the slightest whiff of fraud, researchers clung to large groups of average subjects, who were considered not only less likely to cheat but also less skilled in the techniques of doing so successfully.

Some people have an image of psychically gifted people as dramatic, heavily accented, mysterious; spending their lives in darkened rooms communing mystically with crystal balls. In reality, however, except for their psi abilities, sensitives are generally indistinguishable from the rest of humanity. As Schmeidler observes, "Psychics come male and female; young and old; rich and poor; black, yellow, red, and white; bright and dull; active and passive; fat and thin; leaders and followers."[24] To many Americans, some sensitives' names seem striking, like Lalsingh Harribance, Uri Geller, and Ingo Swann; but these are interspersed with simpler ones, like Pat Price and Eileen Garrett. So even an unusual name is not an occupational characteristic among sensitives.

One example of the kind of results that can be achieved in laboratory work with sensitives—and the kind of complex monitoring equipment currently required by psi researchers—is a 1973 experiment by Gertrude Schmeidler with sensitive Ingo Swann.[25] In this experiment Swann demonstrated his apparent ability to significantly influence temperature recordings made by a highly precise instrument. In five separate sessions his results were superior to chance by odds of 1,000 to 1.

Ingo Swann offers a good example of the normal, everyday exterior most psychics possess. Born in 1933 in Colorado, Swann majored in biology at Westminster College in Salt Lake City, Utah. Astute, widely read, and well known as an artist, Swann worked for a time as a liaison officer for the United Nations in New York; but today his art, writing, and interest in parapsychology occupy all his time. About five feet ten, and slim despite his talent as a gourmet cook, Swann has a jovial round face and twinkling eyes.

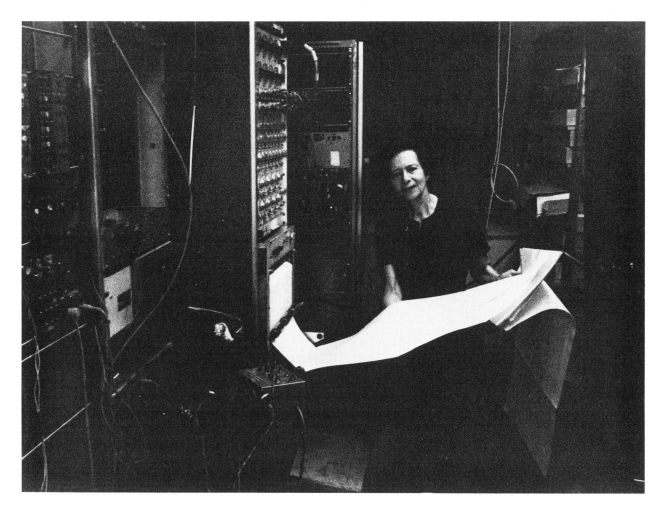

His precise enunciation and dignified manner, however, give an air of total seriousness to any discussion about psi. Swann has been tested at Maimonides Medical Center, at the City University of New York, and at the Stanford Research Institute, the last testing done under a contract with the U.S. National Aeronautics and Space Administration (NASA).

The Schmeidler experiment tested Swann's PK ability. The experimenter wanted to see whether or not Swann could make temperature rise and fall through his psychic abilities alone. To find out, she used four thermisters, extremely precise temperature-monitoring instruments. She connected these instruments to a machine to continuously record temperature changes they detected. Schmeidler and Swann sat together in a room containing the thermisters. Some were exposed; others were protected inside sealed thermos bottles. While watching Swann carefully to make sure he remained seated, Schmeidler would ask him to concentrate on one particular thermister whose location varied from session to session. She would ask him to "make it cooler" or to "make it hotter" in a random order. Swann was given forty-five seconds in which to concentrate on the thermister, and then forty-five seconds to rest before Schmeidler made a new request for temperature change.

Schmeidler found that Swann was able to alter the thermister

Gertrude Schmeidler of City College, the City University of New York, who designed the thermister experiment.

Ingo Swann, the sensitive who attempted to influence the thermister by PK.

45

recording on random command. A particularly striking temperature change took place one day during a rest period. Schmeidler and Swann were relaxing in the laboratory, and Swann was casually "probing" with his mind where the thermister was in a particular sealed thermos bottle. Suddenly Larry Lewis, the assistant experimenter who was watching the readout on a monitoring unit in an adjoining room, noticed a change of nearly one degree during a thirty-second period. Concluding that someone must have opened the thermos bottle, Lewis raced into the laboratory to restore order. There he found Schmeidler and Swann in their accustomed seats, and the thermos bottle still sealed. "What happened?" Lewis exclaimed. Swann admitted he had been mentally probing the target thermister, apparently with success.

After the experiment had been fully developed, Schmeidler asked two students who were not sensitives to try the task of changing temperature readings. One showed significant results, leading Schmeidler to hypothesize, "An ability which is marked in a gifted subject will be found in at least some members of the general population."[26]

When asked four years later about the experiment, Schmeidler said, "Theoretically it seemed impossible to do what we attempted to do with Swann and the thermister. I did not know whether the experiment would be a success or not. When it did occur, it seemed like a miracle. It still does. I don't understand how it happened. I still don't. It just happened."[27]

The results of this experiment indicate that human beings may be able to use PK to influence the recordings of subtle temperature changes. To date, however, no other experimenter has successfully repeated Schmeidler's study.

Psi in Other Species
Experimenters have not confined themselves to the human species. While no conclusive experimental evidence of psi-responsiveness in plants exists, some experimenters believe they have managed to demonstrate the possible existence of psi in animals.

Work with animals offers the experimenter a number of useful advantages. As the writer D. Scott Rogo observes, "Unlike human subjects, animals may not have a built-in censor to keep psi impressions from influencing their behavior. Secondly, animals are probably not prone to boredom or uneasiness when observers are present"[28]—two difficulties that strongly affect human subjects. In addition, researchers assume animals are not subject to autosuggestion—deluding oneself that some psi process is taking place when it is not. Nor are animals considered likely to fake results.

Based on the limited research done with animals to date, the Psi SEARCH consensus was, "Psi may be a universal ability of living beings."[29] There have been animal-centered experiments in which, for example, mice revived faster from anesthesia when concentrated on by a subject,[30] or recovered more quickly from a wound when held between the hands of a sensitive.[31]

Some researchers may have been inspired to study psi in animals, or *anpsi* as psi jargon has it, by the hundreds of stories of

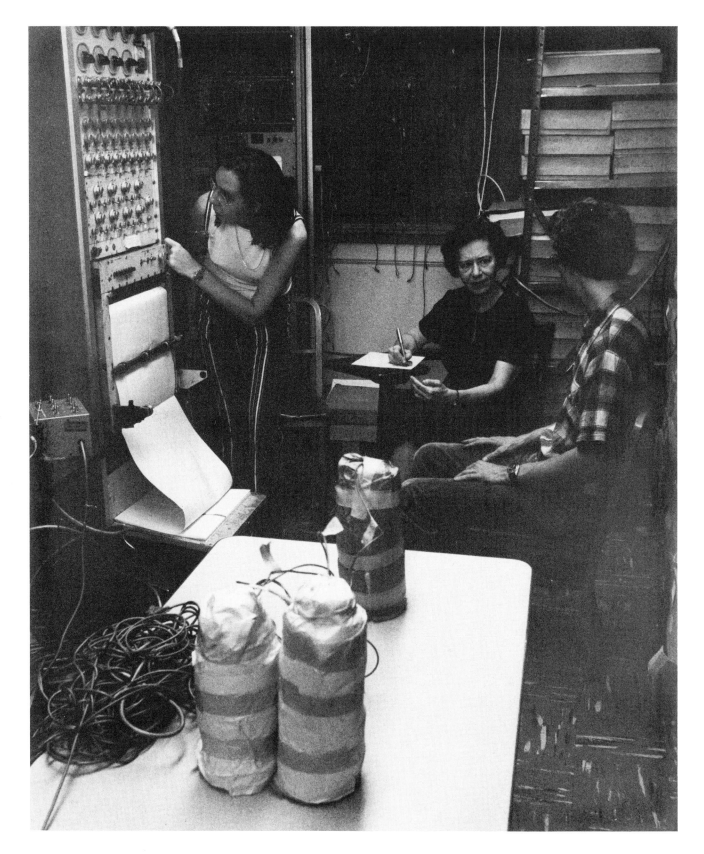

A close-up view of some thermisters of the
type used in the Schmeidler experiment.

animals allegedly managing to track down their owners, even in strange territory. Such stories report on animals' success over long distances and under conditions that appeared to make their ordinary five senses inadequate to handle the task—when, for example, owners had driven over busy highways to get to their destination. J. B. Rhine and Sara Feather studied over fifty cases involving animals,[32] and a number of other researchers have also examined similar stories, but the results were "neither consistent nor overwhelmingly significant."[33]

Laboratory research, on the other hand, appears to have yielded more meaningful results. One experimenter believes that he obtained results that were suggestive of the presence of psi in animals. The experiment involved a researcher-subject named Stuart Blue Harary and a kitten.[34]

The experiment was developed with the cooperation of Robert Morris, presently of the University of California at Santa Barbara, who was a former colleague of Harary's at the Psychical Research Foundation in Durham, North Carolina. The team wanted to test whether out-of-body experience such as Harary said he had occasionally experienced could be detected by a kitten at a distance. Harary would seek to attain the subjective feelings characteristic of an OBE. In an OBE he would feel that he was seeing the world from some specific place outside his physical body—a feeling many claim to have experienced. The OBE experience is at present very poorly understood. The question the experimenters asked was whether a kitten could respond when Harary would attempt to "visit" it during an OBE. They were attempting to get an external indication that something was in fact occurring. The experimental results were considered superior to chance by odds of 100 to 1.

Morris set up his part of the experiment in the following manner. He put Harary's kitten on a floor marked off into ten-inch squares and then he recorded its movements among the numbered squares. Meanwhile, in a building separated from the one containing the kitten by a quarter mile, Harary was surrounded by a cluster of machines to monitor his physiological changes. An EEG measured the activity of the left and right occipital lobes of his brain; an EMG was connected to his chin; his respiration rate, blood volume, and skin resistance were all monitored.

At specific times, Harary attempted to have an out-of-body experience and, during that experience, go to the kitten and calm it. At other times, another experimenter engaged him in active conversation in order to establish times when Harary was definitely not having an OBE, necessary for purposes of experimental control. Morris, watching the kitten in the other building and checking its behavior with a synchronized clock, was not told when Harary was attempting to have an OBE.

The results? At those times when Harary reported feeling out of his body, the usually active kitten became consistently calmer, crossing few or none of the numbered squares. This was not true during control periods.

Morris feels the 100 to 1 experimental results are suggestive of a psi interaction between the kitten and Harary. Later tests, in which Harary attempted to experience being with a hamster, a gerbil, and

Robert Morris, presently of the University of California at Santa Bar bara, who has studied psi in animals.

Experimenter Robert Morris recording the movements of the kitten across a checkerboard of numbered squares.

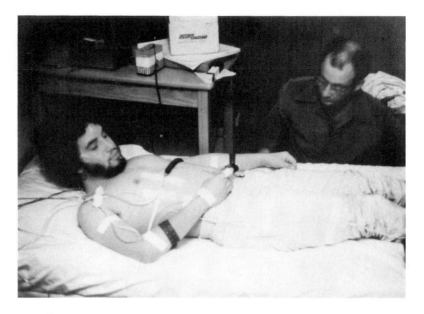

Stuart Blue Harary being prepared for monitoring. (Robert Morris is in the background.)

a snake, gave no consistent evidence of psi interaction between Harary and the animals. Questioned as to why the experiment would work only with the kitten, Morris says that the affinity between Harary and his pet could be responsible, because "Harary didn't really care as much for the other animals."[35]

Morris believes that "there is overall . . . at least some indication that psi in animals may occur in roughly the same ways as it does in humans."[36] While he does not maintain that the experiment clearly demonstrated that Harary did indeed have an out-of-body experience, he does conclude that "some information exchange did take place."[37]

Harary, who has also worked with the Rhines, William Roll, Karlis Osis, and Charles Honorton, remains convinced that the kitten responded to an information exchange effected while he was having an OBE. He says, "The experience is subjectively very much one of being at a separate location from the body. It doesn't necessarily mean that you are separated from the body but that's what it feels like. In that particular experiment with the cat, I would feel as if I were right there with the cat—a very warm, kind of loving feeling of just being with my little friend there at that distant location."[38]

He would probably agree with J. B. von Helmont, who in 1644 wrote: "Every man is capable of influencing his kind at a distance, but generally this force is sleeping in us, suffocated by the body."[39]

Although much work remains to be done on the question of who can use psi, researchers believe some important facts are in hand. Psi seems to be generally distributed among humans, irrespective of age, sex, or intelligence, and may be present among animals as well. Like opera singers, whose voices differ in quality from the average person's, sensitives are psychic virtuosos. But just as nearly everyone can sing a bit, even if only in the shower, so nearly everyone appears to possess some ability to make use of the remarkable phenomenon known as psi.

6.
What Can Psi Communicate?

What can psi communicate? Almost anything.

Just as nearly everyone seems to be able to use psi, so too nearly everything seems to be susceptible to psi transmission or influence. The range of thoughts, events, and things with which subjects have been able to interact in psi testing is remarkably extensive.[1] On the basis of the laboratory work done to date, Robert Van de Castle comments, "Our daily environment is quite possibly teeming with information which we may be processing by psi."[2]

Psi Targets

In laboratory research terms, the *what* of psi interaction is the target subjects are asked to detect (through ESP) or influence (through PK). The target is a key element in providing objective evidence of the existence of psi. It serves the same purpose that a bull's-eye target serves in marksmanship. If people say they are a superb shot with a bow and arrow, their claims can be tested by seeing whether or not they can shoot the arrow into the center of the target. The same relationship exists in psi research. A third party can evaluate the success or failure of subjects' attempted psi interactions by how often they hit or miss the target in an experiment. Scoring is impossible without a target.

As psychologist Robert H. Thouless observes, the existence of the target distinguishes psi from illusion and hallucination,[3] which are purely subjective experiences; the target makes psi an objective experience. This does not mean that psi must always relate to something material. Ellen Messer, for example, may have been relating to Sharon Harper's thoughts about Las Vegas. But if a thought is the target, that thought must be demonstrably related to some objective thing. Again, if Messer was in fact relating to Harper's thoughts, those thoughts arose from a specific and tangible View-Master wheel that Harper studied.

A partial list of the specific targets subjects have been apparently able to influence through PK includes dice,[4] metal balls,[5] photographic film,[6] plants,[7] animals,[8] enzymes,[9] electronic circuits,[10] and perhaps even radioactive particles.[11] Categories of targets that have been successfully perceived through ESP include symbols,[12] words,[13] pictures,[14] numbers,[15] scenes,[16] emotions,[17] and even general personal characteristics.[18]

In the early research experimenters concentrated on selecting target materials that allowed them to compare a subject's results

Psychologist Robert Van de Castle of the University of Virginia Medical School, who did psi research among the Cuna Indians of Panama.

against chance expectations with relative ease. Because they were still seeking irrefutable evidence of psi's existence, researchers were eager to choose targets that were clearcut and mathematically simple to handle.

Consequently, Zener cards and dice became preferred target materials. Using already existing statistical charts, experimenters could quickly ascertain how significant their results with these materials were. Furthermore, test results based on odds of 5 to 1 (cards) or 6 to 1 (dice) could easily be compared from series to series and from laboratory to laboratory in attempts to confirm or disprove various hypotheses about psi. As Gardner Murphy observed, using such materials gave researchers a relatively simple way to compare the effect of such variables as "motivation, the practice effects, the influence of drugs, fatigue, etc."[19]

After much work experimenters felt more certain of their ground, and began to be more flexible in their methods of testing. They decided that they could take into consideration what sort of target content subjects might prefer. Perhaps this new approach would help them locate the perfect psi test that would yield positive results 100 percent of the time. At least it would provide some relief from the sterile stream of dice and cards. As Thouless points out, "A subject may be unable to give a good ESP performance because he is bored with the task he is required to do."[20]

One particular characteristic of PK targets is that most controlled PK experiments involve attempts to influence objects in motion. Researchers have not yet been able to provide a scientifically detailed account of *macro-PK*, the successful movement by PK of heavy, static objects, under laboratory conditions. (However, Graham Watkins and Anita Watkins of Duke University did achieve a laboratory demonstration of apparent PK effect of a compass needle by the sensitive Felicia Parise in 1972.[21]) Nor have researchers been able to document the bending or breaking of metals or other materials of high tensile strength. Even though such incidents have been reported on television and allegedly witnessed by large numbers of people, including some scientists, they have not been corroborated in any scientifically detailed account from controlled laboratory testing.

One professionally attested, single striking example of apparent macro-PK was presented at the proceedings of the Parapsychological Association in Charlottesville, Virginia, in the summer of 1973.[22] It was a report of an incident that occurred at Stanford University.

In a one-time-only demonstration, the sensitive Ingo Swann was asked to attempt to influence a highly complex instrument known as a magnetometer, which monitors changes in magnetic field strength. The magnetometer was located under the Stanford physics building. To keep it free of distracting influences, the Stanford physicists placed it in a superconductive shield in an aluminum container, placed the container within a copper vault, and buried the vault inside five feet of cement deep in the earth. Prior to the experiment, SRI scientists had set up a rapidly decaying magnetic field in the magnetometer. The decay of the magnetic field was being recorded in an SRI lab room. The decay

Forced Choice vs. Free Response

Psi experimenters talk a lot about *forced-choice experiments* and *free-response experiments*. Both are used in testing. If one compares psi experiments to tests given in high school, then a forced-choice experiment is like a multiple-choice exam, and a free-response experiment is like an exam that requires the student to answer in essay form.

In forced-choice experiments, subjects are given a specific number of possible answers, one of which is the target. With Zener cards, for example, subjects know that there are five symbols in the deck and that one of those five symbols is the target.

In free-response experiments, the subject is not given a selection of possible answers from which to choose. Instead, just about anything in the universe could be the target. For example, in an experiment at Stanford Research Institute (discussed in detail in Chapter 8) Uri Geller was asked to draw a picture to correspond to a picture a sender was drawing in another room. The variety of things available to the sender as possible targets was almost limitless.

The main problem experimenters encounter with free-response experiments is trying to judge whether or not there is a clear correspondence between the subject's psi guess and the target. If, for example, the target is an ice-filled glass of ginger ale, and the subject guesses a cold bottle of soda, is the guess correct? Partly correct? Or not correct at all? Independent judging procedures used to evaluate results such as these are highly complex and, to some, not totally reliable because they are based on highly subjective human judgments.

registers on a printout chart as a slow-moving wave similar to the way brain waves read out on an electroencephalogram (EEG).

The demonstration came about in the following manner. The Stanford Research Institute staff working next door to Stanford University had been testing Swann's apparent psi ability. They conceived the idea of pitting Swann's psi against the magnetometer. There the magnetometer was, all locked up and busily putting out its sine-wave signal. Why not see if Swann could use psi to change its readout? The aluminum and copper and cement made the magnetometer appear invulnerable—would Swann be able to penetrate that fortress? Here was a challenge worthy of any sensitive.

The SRI scientists trooped over to the physics department with Swann. Would he please change the sine-wave recording of the magnetic decay? More than one person who heard the question had to hide a smile; it was obviously an impossible task. Yet to the astonishment of those same people, Swann did indeed cause an abrupt change in the magnetic sine-wave recording, possibly indicating that he had altered the decay of the magnetic field.

Then, to show that no other outside source had caused the fluctuation, Swann stopped the wave on the readout chart altogether for forty-five seconds, thus indicating that he had stalled the decay of the magnetic field totally. To top it off, he drew a sketch of what he "saw" the magnetometer's inside to look like, a sketch that Stanford observers said was substantially correct.

Charles Tart and others have pointed out that the Swann demonstration was only a preliminary observation, not an experiment. Furthermore, Swann was free to move about in the vicinity of the monitoring machine. A number of people were milling around the laboratory while the demonstration was in progress.

A number of tests have been devised in which subjects attempted to influence organic processes by psi. One that gave significant results was reported by Anita Watkins and Graham Watkins, in which anesthetized mice were concentrated upon in order to revive them more quickly than a control group.[23] In another, Dolores Krieger, a professor at New York University, demonstrated that the laying-on-of-hands could effect a change in the hemoglobin composition of a person's blood.[24] Enzyme activity in a trypsin solution was accelerated in an experiment with a well-known healer conducted by Sister Mary Justa Smith,[25] researcher and teacher at Rosary Hill College in Buffalo. At McGill University in Montreal, Canada, Dr. Bernard Grad, using the same healer, got results that suggested that the growth of rye seedlings had been speeded up in response to mental influence exercised upon the water given them.[26] These experiments will be further discussed in the next section, SEARCH.

Emotion

The search for improved ESP targets has been every bit as challenging as the search for suitable PK targets. The results? As Rhine puts it, "The range of objects perceptible in ESP is relatively unlimited."[27]

One thing researchers believe they have fairly well established

In the case of forced-choice tests, of course, the results are easier to evaluate. If one of five numbers is chosen as a target, and the subject chooses a number different from the target, the choice is clearly and unambiguously wrong. (Even then, however, if the subject is wrong much more than would be expected by chance, experimenters may conclude the incorrect choice is a result of psi missing.)

The ESP cards designed by Robert Van de Castle for use with the Cuna Indians.

is that it helps in eliciting psi if targets have some emotional relation to the subject. An example can be found in work done by a past president of the Parapsychological Association, Dr. Robert Van de Castle of the Psychiatry Department of the University of Virginia Medical School. He wanted to find out if subjects in a nontechnological culture could produce significant ESP results. Deciding to test Cuna Indians living in Panama's San Blas Islands, Van de Castle felt the standard ESP Zener cards should be modified to have greater meaning to the Cunas. As the French engineer René Warcollier pointed out in 1938, "In spontaneous telepathy the message is almost always emotional and affective."[28] Why not make the test targets closer to what apparently prevailed in real-life situations? Van de Castle, therefore, made "colored pictures the size of playing cards depicting five objects that would be familiar to Cunas: a jaguar in a jungle setting, an underwater view of a shark, a conch shell on sand, a large canoe with a sail, and a propeller airplane in the sky."[29] Van de Castle believes the results of his field study "offer solid evidence "[30] that positive ESP results can also be obtained from nontechnological cultures.

Russell Targ (left) and Harold Puthoff (right) of the Stanford Research Institute, designers of the flashing lights experiment.

Another experimenter reasoned that if a single meaningful target worked well, perhaps a double-barreled approach would work better. Thelma Moss of the Neuropsychiatric Institute of UCLA tested this possibility by using double targets consisting of combined auditory and visual information in an attempt to produce strong psi. In one example from her experiment, done with psychologist J. A. Gengerelli, a sender heard a recording of a funeral dirge through headphones while watching slides of the assassination of President Kennedy. This and other double-impact targets yielded highly significant results.[31] The Psi SEARCH advisors, noting the high emotional content of the targets Moss used, suggest that her results indicate that emotional content aids psi information transmission.[32]

Flashing Lights

Some researchers think that humans may be processing psi information throughout both their waking and sleeping existences. Van de Castle says, "I think that is happening much more frequently to many more people than we are aware of."[33] One particularly intriguing experiment with a rather unusual target does indicate that people respond to psi stimuli even when they are not consciously aware of doing so. The experiment in question was done at the Stanford Research Institute by Russell Targ and Harold Puthoff, both of whom are physicists. They decided to test whether or not a subject would demonstrate an unconscious physical response to a light being randomly flashed into a sender's eyes in another room.[34] Their results were just barely significant (about 20 to 1).

Like Van de Castle's modified Zener cards and Moss' double-impact targets, the flashing lights were chosen as targets because of their emotional (as well as physiological) impact. Having powerful lights flashed into one's eyes is not pleasant. The researchers chose this abrasive kind of target in the belief that it approximated the kind of unpleasant emotional overtones that often accompany spontaneous psi experiences in daily life.

Puthoff and Targ monitored the subject's brain-wave response to the flashing lights with the help of an EEG machine. They found

How the Flashing-Light Experiment Worked

Puthoff and Targ's experiment with flashing lights worked as follows. The subject was introduced to the sender and was told that lights would be flashed at randomly chosen times into the sender's eyes. The subject was further told that he would have no way to tell (through the use of his five senses) when the lights were flashed at the sender. The subject was kept several rooms apart from the sender so that no light flashes could be seen by the subject.

During twenty-four randomly chosen periods, the light-flashing device was shined into the sender's eyes. All the subject did was relax and permit the experimenters to monitor his brain waves by means of an EEG. The subject was explicitly instructed that his conscious mind was not involved at all—that he was not to try to guess when the lights were flashed.

The experimenters on some occasions also used a buzzer that sounded in the two rooms where the subject and the sender were. The subject was told that when the buzzer sounded, sometimes lights would be flashed into the sender's eyes and sometimes they would not. Its purpose was simply to alert him that something *might* be happening to the sender. The buzzer sounded thirty-six times in a series, twenty-four times just before the light flashed and twelve times when it did not.

The subject's EEG was significantly less powerful at those times when light was flashed into the sender's eyes than when the warning buzzer sounded and the sender was *not* subjected to the flashing lights.

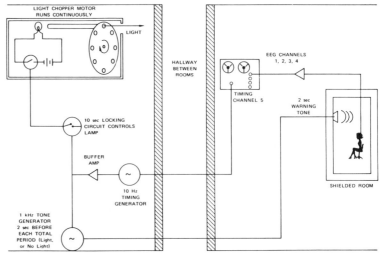

LIGHT CHOPPER MOTOR
RUNS CONTINUOUSLY

LIGHT

HALLWAY
BETWEEN
ROOMS

EEG CHANNELS
1, 2, 3, 4

TIMING
CHANNEL 5

2 sec
WARNING
TONE

10 sec LOCKING
CIRCUIT CONTROLS
LAMP

SHIELDED ROOM

BUFFER
AMP

10 Hz
TIMING
GENERATOR

1 kHz TONE
GENERATOR
2 sec BEFORE
EACH TOTAL
PERIOD (Light,
or No Light)

REMOTE SENSING EEG EXPERIMENT

A diagram of the flashing lights experiment. Note that the lights were battery operated.

One curious incident occurred during the experimental series. There were seven runs in the course of the experiment, and the changes in brain waves occurred in all but one. In that one the experimenters told the receiver that there would not be anyone in the remote room looking at the strobe light, and the receiver's brain waves showed no significant changes during that run.

Later, however, as another run was starting, a visitor suggested that the experimenters remove the sender from the remote room without telling the subject. In that run the drop in brain waves was one of the strongest in the series, just as though the sender was still in the room.[35]

The implication is that there was a psychological element to the brain-wave response, and when the subject was told that there was no sender, her psi response was blocked. But when she believed a sender was present, she responded to the flashing strobe even though, in fact, there was no one in the room to be affected by the light.

There was one other interesting result. As part of the experiment, the subject was asked to press a button to indicate whether she thought the light was flashing during each of the trials. An analysis of her guesses showed that they were at chance level; that is, she was not able to consciously tell whether or not the light was on, nor was there any psi in her conscious guesses. This seems to mean that the psi response was only in her brain waves, at a physiological level, and outside of her conscious awareness.

decreases in the subject's brain-wave response that significantly corresponded to the times when bright light was flashed into the sender's eyes. The subject and the sender were put in widely separated rooms so there was no way for the subject to know when the lights were being flashed at the sender.

Many psi lay interest groups maintain that ESP originates in the right hemisphere of the brain. Some of these groups cite the flashing lights experiment as proof. Puthoff and Targ do not agree. They are careful to point out that the results of their experiment do *not* show "that the brain (or the right hemisphere) is the organ of paranormal functioning, the 'seat of the soul,' or anything like that."[36] They do believe, however, that their experiment indicates people may be unconsciously receiving and reacting to psi information, perhaps frequently.

One researcher who agrees with Puthoff and Targ is Rex Stanford, who has written, "Spontaneous psi events occur without the conscious intention of the experiencing person."[37] He suggests, as two possible examples of the unconscious operation of psi in daily life, always finding a parking place and knowing from whom a telephone call is coming even before the telephone rings. Because his theories, developed while he was Assistant Professor of Psychology at St. John's University, in Jamaica, New York, have not been fully tested in the laboratory, they will be discussed in the next section, SEARCH.

Results of experimental research continue to widen the demonstrated range of what psi can communicate. The cumulative results of that research suggest that a broad gamut of human experience may be open to psi interaction. As Stanford says, psi "may be much more frequent and integral in the scheme of things than we have imagined."[38] It may be that psi is to our five senses what peripheral vision is to our sight, expanding the breadth and depth of information available to us without our conscious knowledge.

7.
When Does a Psi Exchange Occur?

A psi exchange can happen just about any time—and psi exchanges may be taking place *all* the time. As the writer D. Scott Rogo puts it, "ESP does occur continually, although we are hardly ever aware of it."[1] Louisa Rhine thinks that people become aware of psi only when something happens that they cannot explain away; the rest of the time psi exchanges remain below the conscious level of their minds.[2]

Psi and Time

Scientists in psi laboratories have done a considerable amount of work examining the relationship between psi and time. Perhaps their most startling discovery is that it does not appear to be necessary for a subject and a target to exist at the same time. Some experimental work indicates that a subject can gain information about a target before that target even exists. In other words, people seem to be able to predict future events.

The possibility that people are able to know the future through psi is so revolutionary that many find it the most difficult of all aspects of psi to accept. Even people who have long accepted psi's existence can be uncomfortable with the precognitive facet of the phenomenon. An example is George Washington University's Gardner Murphy, one of the United States' best known theoreticians in psychology. Murphy has devoted a great deal of time and effort to his attempts to integrate psychology and parapsychology. Yet in an early survey of psi, Murphy could not bring himself to discuss precognition. He avoided doing so, he said, because of the "difficult or, indeed, 'outrageous' observations that have to be dealt with."[3]

Many would agree that the very idea of communication between a person who exists and a target that does not is indeed outrageous. And yet this does appear to happen in psi testing. Consider the trial of the Ganzfeld technique at Maimonides involving Ellen Messer. Messer began to see images of cowboys and nightclub dancers *before* Sharon Harper saw the View-Master wheel of Las Vegas. Honorton noted this same seemingly precognitive tendency with a number of other subjects in the same experimental series.[4] That tendency was simply an accidental byproduct of Honorton's work. Several other experiments, however, have intentionally focused on the possibility that subjects can interact successfully with a target before it exists. One such experiment, designed by Jarl Fahler, Director of Finland's Institute for Parapsychology, and Karlis Osis, a former president of the

D. Scott Rogo, who has written extensively on the history of the investigation of psychic phenomena.

Karlis Osis, shown during an experiment. With Jarl Fahler, Osis tested the effects of hypnosis on precognitive psi.

Parapsychological Association, was conducted under a grant from the Parapsychology Foundation in New York.[5] It succeeded in demonstrating that subjects apparently can predict the future.

Fahler and Osis asked subjects under hypnosis to try to predict in what order the numbers one through ten would be randomly listed on a sheet the next day. Further, each was asked to indicate whenever he or she felt *certain* a specific prediction would be correct. These predictions were filed and locked away by one of the experimenters. The next day an assistant, who had not been present when the subjects had made their predictions, listed the numbers in random order on a sheet and then compared them to the list predicted by the subjects.

In those cases when the subjects had been certain about their prediction, the numbers matched the random list at odds of 50 million to 1 over chance. How could a subject be certain about an event that had not yet happened, and be so often correct in that certainty? Was it precognition? Or did the subject somehow influence the subsequent randomizing process through PK?

Karlis Osis recalls with considerable pleasure the experimental results he and Jarl Fahler obtained. He calls the statistical significance of their experiment one of the highest ever reported by any scientist investigating precognition. Osis attributes this success to a combination of two elements: one is that the subjects were hypnotized; the other is that they enjoyed a particularly warm and supportive relationship with Fahler. Osis says, "Hypnosis alone was not enough to cause a high score. But when that special relationship was added to it, then subjects were able to do very, very well."[6] And what they did, it appears, was predict the future.

Another experiment that tested precognitive psi was done by Stanley Krippner, Montague Ullman, and Charles Honorton at the Maimonides Medical Center dream laboratory.[7] It was the first laboratory test of something often reported by both sensitives and ordinary people: that they had dreams that accurately predicted future events. The Maimonides team decided to see if this ability could be demonstrated in the laboratory. They used Malcolm Bessent, an English sensitive with a history of spontaneous precognitive experiences. The experimenters asked Bessent to dream about an experience that had not yet been selected. Instead, it would be chosen by a random procedure and arranged for him the next day. According to outside judges, Bessent did this successfully several times, yielding results 5,000 to 1 over chance.

The results of the work done with Bessent indicate that psi may interact with target events even before they are created. Experimenters are not sure how, in the case of Bessent, this happened. Did he in fact predict something that not only had not happened but had not even been planned? Or could the experimenter who designed the subsequent experiences have been influenced in some psi way by Bessent's dreams, even though he had no knowledge of what those dreams were about? As Cicero reportedly speculated many centuries ago, "Human minds when set free by sleep or in detached states of excited derangement perceive things which minds involved with the body cannot see."[8]

Honorton recalls the results as being emotionally stimulating to him as an experimenter as well as to Bessent as the subject:

> Intellectually at least, I was pretty comfortable with the idea of precognition when we did the study. I expected that it would work, that he would be able to pick up on the experiences that would be created for him the following morning. However, as the study progressed, some of the correspondences were so striking that the experiment had an emotional effect on me that I didn't expect. It made precognition something more than an abstract concept—it made it something that I could see.[9]

Successful Subjects
As researchers continue to search for the perfect psi experiment, they attempt to identify which variables enhance the likelihood of psi occurrence. While spontaneous psi may, it seems, occur at almost any time, when a researcher tries to elicit it in the laboratory on demand it is helpful to know when conditions favor its appearance. This question of when psi occurs has probably attracted more research than any other aspect of psi.

Some of the experiments already covered in this book iden-

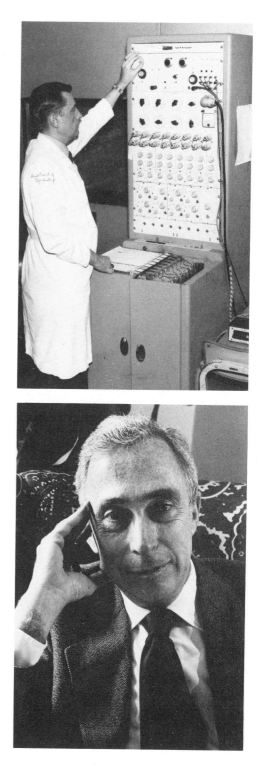

Stanley Krippner (top) and Montague Ullman (bottom), who tested precognitive psi at the Maimonides Medical Center's dream laboratory.

tified certain personal characteristics of successful psi subjects. Schmeidler feels the results of her work indicate that successful subjects are often possessed of a friendly and outgoing personality and are comfortable with the idea that psi exists. Honorton and Harper felt that their better Ganzfeld subjects were capable of good visual imagery ability and were able to easily recall their dreams. Fahler and Osis found that subjects' confidence in their hunches was important. And Rhine placed emphasis on subjects' interest in the experiment.

Helpful Conditions

Other experiments already described identified certain experimental conditions that appear to enhance psi interaction. Schmidt, in his RNG work, felt good rapport with the experimenter was important, as did Fahler and Osis. Roll and Klein emphasized the support of a person acting as a sender. Van de Castle designed targets that were emotionally involving, as did the team of Krippner, Ullman, and Honorton in their experiment with Bessent. Tart was careful to give his subjects immediate feedback as to their success or failure in psi guessing.

Two other experimental conditions that seem to help elicit psi will be seen in experiments that will be discussed in the following chapter. One is to not force subjects to respond to every target but instead to permit them to respond only when they feel certain of their hunch.[10] The other is to make the subjects "feel they have permission to use their latent paranormal abilities."[11] In other words, that it is "safe" to be psychic.

In addition to personality characteristics and experimental conditions, experimenters have isolated another factor that appears to affect psi response: the subject's mental state. Professor J. Gaither Pratt of the University of Virginia Medical Center speculates that "psychical experiences may depend on special states of mind."[12] One experiment that indicates that relaxation facilitates psi results was done by Dr. Lendell W. Braud and Dr. William Braud at the University of Houston. They tested a number of college students to see if relaxation techniques could produce improved psi response.[13] Their results showed that a relaxed state was superior to a tense state at odds of 1,000 to 1 over chance.

The Brauds divided their student subjects into two groups, each with the same proportion of males and females. One group was told that they would have better psi results if they "relaxed," and the experimenters played a taped recording to help them to relax. The other group was told that to "be tense" would help them, and the experimenters played a tension-inducing tape. Each subject was asked to describe an art print that an experimenter was concentrating upon in a nearby room. A physiological check of the subjects' muscular relaxation was made by an electromyograph (EMG), and they were also asked later whether they had felt relaxed or not. The relaxed subjects had significantly better results in a test of psi than did those who were told to be tense.

Thus the Brauds reconfirmed that ". . . the evidence is strikingly consistent and highly suggestive of the important role of relaxation in successful psi functioning."[14] William Braud be-

Dreams that Came True

The precognitive test designed for Malcolm Bessent by the Maimonides group asked the subject to dream about an experience that would not actually be designed or take place until the following day. In other words, he was asked to have a precognitive dream. The experiment was based on the theory that subjects are more likely to receive psi information *if the content of that information is emotionally stimulating in some way.* Spurred by this theory, the Maimonides experimenters went to remarkable lengths in order to render as powerful as possible the multisensory experience Bessent was to try to predict in his dreams. The same theory underlay the SRI experiment discussed in Chapter 5, where the target was bright lights shined into a sender's eyes.

The basic experimental procedure was quite simple. Bessent slept in the Maimonides dream laboratory. His brain-wave patterns and rapid eye movements were monitored. He was awakened after each dream period (revealed by particular brain-wave patterns and rapid eye movement of his closed eyes) and his report on the content of his dreams was tape-recorded.

When Bessent awoke in the morning, a research assistant not acquainted with the content of Bessent's dreams selected a key word by random process from a list of topics frequently dreamed about. The assistant then chose an art print (from a pool of several hundred prints) that represented the word selected. His job was to create a multisensory environment based on the art print for Bessent to experience, including sounds, tastes, smells, tactile sensations, and visual elements.

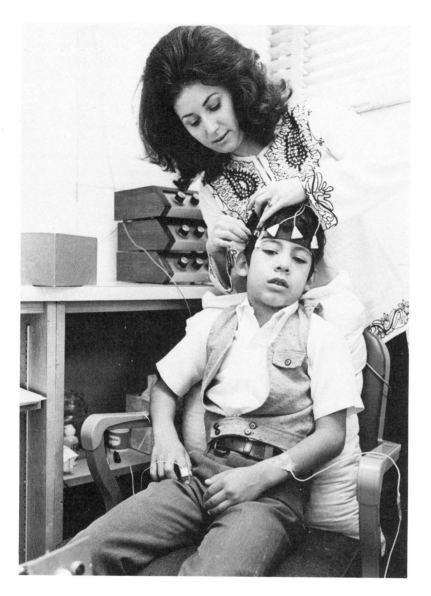

The key feature of this experiment was that Bessent actually experienced an emotionally stimulating environment related to the art print. The experiment was designed to test whether or not the emotional impact of that environment would enhance the predictive accuracy of Bessent's dreams.

The experiment was repeated eight times, using a different print as the target each time. Then independent judges were asked to attempt to blind match each set of art prints against the corresponding transcript of Bessent's dreams the night before. Which print from the set matched the transcript of his dreams? Five of the eight dream descriptions were matched by the judges to the art print on which the subsequent day's experience had been based, yielding 5,000 to 1 odds.

One example of the kind of emotionally stimulating experience the assistant designed came to be called "Parka-Hood." One of the art prints chosen had been of an Eskimo walrus hunter wearing a parka. The theme of the print, obviously, was coldness. In order to help Bessent experience this theme as vividly as possible, the assistant placed Bessent between two electric fans, dropped ice cubes down his back, and plunged his hand into ice water.

The experimenters believed that having Bessent undergo such a powerful, multisensory experience would reinforce and thus improve his potential precognitive abilities.

lieves their experiment demonstrated that "psi is a subtle thing and is easily overwhelmed by noise or distractions—such as the noise our own bodies generate."[15] Braud says their experiment helped successful subjects to lower their personal noise by reducing muscular tension, and so to detect the weak psi signal. In fact, the correlation between relaxation and psi success was so clear that the experimenters found they could accurately predict how successful a particular subject would be according to the degree of relaxation demonstrated on the EMG test.[16] "This important finding," say the Psi SEARCH advisors about relaxation, "has become one of the major new research directions in parapsychology."[17]

Some experimenters have moved beyond simple relaxation techniques to explore further effects of what are called altered states of consciousness. Whether dreaming, hypnotized, or simply unusually relaxed, subjects in such a state are mentally quiet and able to give their full attention to their own mental imagery. (As was shown in the Ellen Messer story, psi often seems to appear in the form of mental images.)

Miss Z and OBEs

Charles Tart's experiment with Miss Z worked as follows: On four successive nights Miss Z came to Tart's sleep lab to attempt to have an OBE. She was asked to do so while resting on a cot in the laboratory. In order

Researchers have long recognized that the dream state can sometimes yield psi information. Freud, well aware of this, wrote, "Sleep seems to be especially suitable for the reception of telepathic communication."[18] Some years ago, researchers discovered that when people dream, their eyes make rapid movements behind their closed eyelids. A technique developed to monitor the rapid eye movements (REMs) that accompany dreams allows researchers to awaken subjects immediately after they have finished dreaming. Sleepers so awakened are often able to give full and vivid accounts of what they have just dreamed. Despite this development, studying psi through dreams is still a time-consuming process, and requires expensive equipment and staff to appropriately monitor dreaming subjects.

Hypnosis, another altered state of consciousness, has been used by many researchers as a means of getting some extremely high positive psi results. In a review of these studies, Honorton and Krippner state that "Hypnosis provides one of the few presently available techniques for affecting the level of psi test performance."[19] Not all experimenters are skilled in hypnosis, however, and not all psi subjects are good subjects for hypnosis.

Drugs and alcohol have also come in for a share of psi testing. Results that have been obtained to date indicate that, with rare individual exceptions, they are not psi facilitators. Pratt has written that limited experiments with drugs give observers no reason to expect "that drugs provide any master key to unlock hidden ESP powers."[20]

Relaxation seems to be the least complicated and most psi-effective mental state for experimenters to encourage in their subjects. In attempting to help their subjects relax, as the Brauds did, experimenters frequently ask them to use some form of a progressive relaxation or meditation technique. They may use tape recordings of suggested steps leading toward relaxation, rely upon the subject's own autosuggestion to relax, or simply ask the subject to expect success and let go of tension.[21] In each case the scientists are attempting to help their subjects achieve a "relaxed, passive state of mind."[22] In this state, the faint whisper that is psi can sometimes be heard with surprising clarity.

The Moment of Psi Exchange

A final question is, exactly when does a psi exchange take place? Until recently, the answer depended on the subjective evaluation of experimenters and subjects. But now scientists have begun to make use of new monitoring techniques and equipment as a means of detecting some unconscious, physiological change that may betray when a person experiences psi. By helping to pinpoint precisely when psi occurs, the scientists hope to gain a better understanding of exactly how psi is transmitted.[23] One example of such an experiment was seen in the SRI flashing-light experiment described in Chapter 6. Another was performed by Charles Tart of the University of California at Davis. In it Tart monitored a sensitive who attempted to discover a concealed five-digit number while having an out-of-body experience.[24] The sensitive, identified by Tart only as "Miss Z," managed to do so successfully, a 100,000 to 1 feat.

Charles Tart reading a computer print-out measuring Miss Z's brain waves.

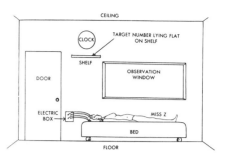

A diagram of the experiment in which Miss Z correctly reported a concealed five-digit number.

Tart's was the first truly controlled laboratory experiment attempting to investigate a reported out-of-body experience. This is the same experience attempted in the experiment by Robert Morris and his colleagues, in which the sensitive Stuart Blue Harary "visited his kitten," described in Chapter 5. Spurred by descriptions he had heard and read of such experiences, Tart wondered if it would be possible "to ask what is going on there . . . and come up with some interesting results."[25]

The purpose of Tart's experiment was to see if the OBEs Miss Z reported having could be repeated in the laboratory. By asking her to identify the hidden number, Tart was attempting to obtain some objective evidence to support her claimed OBEs. About the results of the experiment, the Psi SEARCH advisors say, "The implication of the study is that Miss Z's brain-wave patterns appeared to be distinctive when she reported having been out of body. These studies warrant further study."[26]

It may be that humans are continually using psi to scan their environment. Most of the time they may be doing so unconsciously, just as they ignore the steady whir of an air conditioner. But sometimes, when they make their minds very still, or when the message is unusually strong, they take conscious note of psi information. Perhaps this occasional alertness parallels the ancient survival instinct evolved to protect people when they sleep, letting them snore peacefully next to a thundering waterfall, but bringing them instantly awake at the sound of a single stick snapping in the undergrowth.

to obtain a profile of any physiological changes in Miss Z during a reported OBE, Tart attached wires to her from machines that monitored her brain-wave patterns, rapid eye movement, basal skin resistance, galvanic skin resistance, heart rate, and blood volume.

Tart also chose a different five-digit number each night (from a mathematical table of random numbers) and wrote it on a slip of paper. After Miss Z was wired to the monitoring machines, the experimenter placed the paper on a shelf 5½ feet above her. He asked Miss Z to try to read the number during an OBE. The monitoring wires were so short that Miss Z could not get up off the cot in order to look at the number in the ordinary way without breaking off the recording process. Each night Miss Z was asked to sleep until she felt she had had an OBE. Then she was to try to wake up and tell Tart what she had seen.

The first night nothing significant happened. The second night Miss Z reported having an OBE. She said that while "floating" she saw a clock on the wall above the shelf (which could not be seen from where she lay on the cot), and that the time shown on the clock was 3:15 A.M. At that exact time the machine readouts showed distinctly unusual brain-wave patterns, but there was no evidence of the kind of rapid eye movements that usually accompany dreams. A similar correspondence was noted on the third night, when she reported, the time on the clock face as 3:35 A.M.

On the fourth night Miss Z correctly reported the concealed number: 25132. She reported the time as between 5:50 and 6:00 A.M. At 5:57 A.M. her brain-wave readouts showed the strange characteristic patterns noted on previous occasions, only more pronounced.

8.
Where Can Psi Occur?

Where can psi occur? Apparently anywhere.
Psi seems to be basically unaffected by location. As René Warcollier wrote, spontaneous psi exchange has been noted in "... churches, concert halls, theatres, conferences, public gatherings, and between persons living in the same house, in the same locality, in the same country."[1] This is apparently true of psi in the laboratory as well.

Psi in the Individual
One of the more interesting questions involving psi and place has to do with the internal world rather than the external one. That is, where does psi occur within the individual? Researchers agree that psi occurs without our conscious awareness,[2] although they are not in agreement on how this process is achieved. The whole process is apparently so subtle that, as has already been described, people can be completely unaware of psi exchange even when it is demonstrably taking place.

The reason for this, according to Louisa Rhine, is that the faint whisper that is psi is often obliterated or distorted when it travels from the unconscious into the conscious mind: "When ESP messages are transferred to consciousness, the threshold presents a barrier. Often ... only part of the message gets through—frequently only the emotional component."[3]

As researchers press their investigation into the nature of psi, from time to time they bypass conscious manifestations of psi exchange, choosing instead to focus on evidence of psi transmission in the unconscious. The SRI researchers, for example, monitored subjects' brain waves in an attempt to discern their psi response to lights being flashed in senders' eyes. As was described in Chapter 6, they found a clear correlation between changes in the subjects' brain-wave patterns and times when lights were flashed at the senders, even though the subjects were totally unaware of these changes on a conscious level.

Psi in the Laboratory
These investigations are possible, of course, only because psi can be elicited under laboratory conditions. Expensive and complex monitoring equipment would be virtually useless to researchers if they were forced to seek psi on a haphazard basis, trundling EEG machines down the street in the hope that they might stumble on an instance of spontaneous psi.

One experiment that investigated unconscious response to psi and could be conducted only in the laboratory was performed by E. Douglas Dean and Carroll B. Nash at the Newark College of Engineering.[4] The experiment was a forerunner of the SRI flashing-light test. The two researchers found that psi may affect subjects' bodily processes without their knowledge that anything at all is taking place. Their experiment used names familiar to a subject as targets to trigger psi response. The subject's response was evaluated through changes in peripheral blood volume.

The experiment worked as follows. A subject was asked to simply relax quietly in a room. His blood volume was monitored by a special sensor, known as a finger–cup plethysmograph, which detects minute changes in blood volume in the small vessels close to the skin responsible for blushing or paling. In a second room, carefully separated from the room containing the subject, Dean, acting as sender, concentrated on a series of cards, one by one. Five cards were blank; five showed names taken from the telephone directory; five contained names of personal friends of Dean's, unknown to the subject; and five contained names emotionally important to the subject, such as a spouse, a child, or a close friend.

The subject did not know when names were being sent nor which names would be sent. He showed significant changes in blood volume when names important to him were concentrated upon, changes that differed from variations at all other times at odds of 50 to 1 over chance. One name called forth an unusually high response. It was the name of the subject's boss. It appeared forty-three times in a series of ten experiments, and the subject's blood volume indicated a physiological response thirty-eight out of the forty-three times Dean concentrated on that name.

The results indicate that people may react physically to psi information even though they may be completely unaware of doing so. To some people this concept is startling, and even a bit disquieting. If correct, it would mean that people are subject to many influences of which they may be completely unaware.

Dean believes that one possible feature of psi indicated by the experimental results is that senders can be effective even if they are unaware of the significance of what they are sending.[5] The only names with which the sender was familiar were the five he himself submitted. He did not know which of the other names were from the telephone book and which had been submitted by the subject. Therefore, he treated each name equally, not placing any special emphasis on the names important to the subject.

Unlike the SRI flashing-light experiment, the subject was not given any indication of when Dean was actually concentrating on a name. In a second series, Dean turned on a light in the subject's room to alert him that a name was being sent. The subject claimed the light interfered with his concentration, distracted him, and made it impossible for him to relax. The results under this procedure were very poor, another possible indication that relaxation is an important component of psi transmission.

There is one other curious note. Dean ran a similar ten-day series of experiments with another subject, an extremely insecure student who was in considerable awe of the experimenter, view-

E. Douglas Dean of the Newark College of Engineering, who tested some physiological aspects of unconscious psi response.

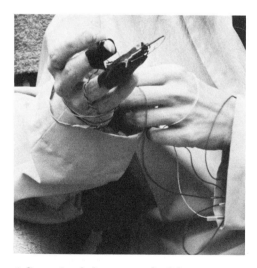

A fingertip plethysmograph of the cup type used in the Dean and Nash experiment.

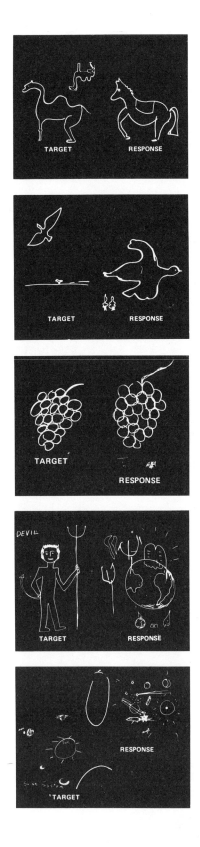

Experimental targets and Uri Geller's responses, from the Stanford Research Institute experiment.

ing him as an authority figure. On nine of the days, the subject responded only to the names Dean brought in, showing no response to the names he himself submitted. On just one of the ten days, the pattern was reversed, and the subject reacted to his own names, showing no response to Dean's names. After the experimental series was over, Dean asked the subject what was special about the one day when the pattern had been reversed. He learned that that day had been the subject's birthday and that he was looking forward to a party in his honor scheduled for that evening. Dean believes that this had given the subject a sense of his own importance, making it possible for him to overcome his insecurity and his awe for Dean, and may account for the reversed experimental results.[6]

Technology available to researchers improves psi testing. At Duke University, psychologist Ed Kelly and John Artley of the Department of Engineering have devised special equipment for psi testing, including mechanical randomization of targets, automated scoring, computer analysis, a memory bank, and other devices for handling psi data. Kelly says he hopes to make the Duke facility a processing service center for many researchers.[7]

In addition to these secondary advantages, a laboratory has one primary advantage as a place for psi testing. This is, of course, the tight controls that can be achieved in a laboratory situation, making the laboratory the place where the surest tests of psi are possible. One person who has been tested under these conditions is the famous Israeli entertainer and sensitive Uri Geller. Two tests conducted at the Stanford Research Institute appear to confirm that Geller has exceptional clairvoyant ability.[8]

In the first test Geller was asked to make drawings to match those being made by an experimenter several rooms away. The experimenter randomly selected dictionary nouns and made appropriate simple line drawings of them. The pairs of drawings made by the sender and Geller were matched by outside judges at odds of 30 million to 1 over chance. An example of the close similarity between the sender's drawings and Geller's approximations is seen in the case of one of the sender's drawings, a cluster of grapes. Geller not only drew a cluster of grapes in response but also drew the same number of clustered grapes as the sender—twenty-four.

In a second test Geller was asked to guess which face of a die was up in an opaque box shaken by the experimenter. Geller, who was not permitted to touch the box, was told he could decline to choose when he felt uncertain. The die was shaken ten times, and Geller chose to respond eight of those times. Each time that he chose to respond he was correct, giving a result at odds of 17,500,000 to 1 over chance.

Just because experiments have been conducted in a laboratory, however, does not mean that everyone agrees with the results. When Russell Targ and Harold Puthoff published a paper describing their two tests with Geller in the prestigious British journal *Nature*, many members of the scientific community bristled. One, Joseph Scanlon, published a lengthy article in the *New Scientist*, in which he suggested that Targ and Puthoff had not eliminated the possibility of fraud.[9] He said that Geller could have received

coded information about the drawings from a conspirator through a radio implanted in one of Geller's teeth, and pointed out that Geller had not agreed to be x-rayed prior to testing (the x-ray would have revealed a tooth radio, if present). As for the die results, he said that it is possible to buy a die for under $100 that radios which face is up. He speculated that such a die could have been substituted through sleight-of-hand for the SRI die prior to testing.

Despite these charges, the Parapsychological Association representatives who worked on the Psi SEARCH exhibit agreed that the Geller results support the notion that a person may be able to use psi to obtain highly accurate information.[10] Most—but not all—believe that the conditions in the laboratory were sufficiently controlled to offer probable confirmation of Geller's alleged clairvoyant abilities. His possible metal-bending abilities, however, have not yet been tested under similar rigid conditions. They will be discussed in more detail in Chapter 12.

Psi at a Distance

One of the questions a number of researchers have considered is the effect of distance on successful psi transmission. That is, does the faint whisper of psi get weaker as it has farther to travel? J. B. Rhine thinks not. He has written, ". . . distance is of no importance in ESP success."[11] Michael Scriven agrees, saying, "In general, we have no evidence which would enable us to say that there is a falling off in ESP performance with distance."[12]

Just how great the distances can be between subjects and targets has not been definitively studied. Rhine's Pearce–Pratt results, discussed in Chapter 3, were considered particularly striking among the early psi tests because the sender and receiver were in two separate buildings. The Morris kitten experiment, discussed in Chapter 5, separated the sensitive from his pet by a quarter mile.

One very long-range test of psi transmission was done by Douglas Dean over an eight-thousand-mile distance.[13] A sender concentrated on a series of names, and a subject's blood volume was monitored to see if he showed a physiological reaction to the

Pamela de Maigret (on the right), who participated in a test of psi over eight thousand miles.

names that were important to him. Dean acted as the subject, assisted by C. A. Maier of the Jung Institute, who served as the experimenter. Both men were in Zurich, Switzerland. The sender was Pamela de Maigret, who was on a Smithsonian Explorers' Association expedition off the coast of Florida. Dean asked de Maigret to attempt the transmission while scuba diving in the Atlantic Ocean. The U.S. Navy cooperated with the experimenters by recording the precise times of attempted psi transmission by de Maigret to Dean.

The results? Despite the eight thousand miles, and despite the sender's being under water, the same significant changes in blood volume were detected in the subject when and only when the sender concentrated on names important to the subject.

Another imaginative experiment involving both distance and laboratory controls was devised by the Stanford Research Institute physicists Harold Puthoff and Russell Targ using a particularly well-liked sensitive who died in 1975, named Patrick H. Price.[14] At one time police commissioner of Burbank, California, Price was well respected in the field of psi investigation.

In this *remote viewing* experiment Price was asked to describe where a car had been driven thirty minutes after it left the laboratory. In a series of nine trials, Price's descriptions matched the actual destinations—according to independent judges—at odds over chance of 560,000 to 1.

The experiment worked like this. Price would relax, supervised, in a room in the laboratory. At the same time a team of experimenters would drive away from the laboratory in a car, stop, and open an envelope that had been randomly chosen from among ten sealed envelopes, each containing different instructions as to an ultimate destination. Then they would drive to the

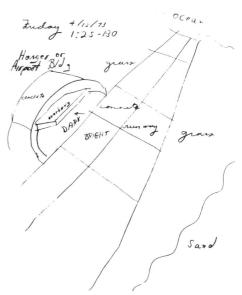

(Left) Airport in Colombia used as remote viewing target. (Right) Sketch produced by subject in Menlo Park, California.

destination described in the envelope. Back at the lab, no one had any way of knowing to which destination the people in the car would drive. This would be known only when the car returned. Thirty minutes after the car had left the laboratory, the experimenter would ask Price to describe where the car had been driven. And he managed to do so to a remarkable extent, achieving the 560,000 to 1 odds already mentioned.

The experimenters write, "Price's ability to describe correctly buildings, docks, roads, gardens and so on, including structural materials, colors, ambience and activity, sometimes in great detail, indicated the functioning of a remote perceptual ability."[15]

The results of this study, which has been successfully repeated with a number of ordinary visitors to SRI, indicate that psi may enable a person to get information from complex and distant targets. However, some critics find the data inadequate.

The influence range of PK has not been as thoroughly studied to date. Gertrude Schmeidler has pointed out that in the experiment she did with Ingo Swann (discussed in Chapter 5), the area around the target thermister registered rises and falls in temperature along with the target.[16]

Gardner Murphy has noted that, in psi experimentation, extending the distance between subject and target from several feet to separate rooms did not reduce, but rather increased, the effect when distance was directly tested.[17] Researchers agree that more experimentation is called for in this area to see just what limits—if any—exist with PK transmission.

The meaning of all this appears to be that psi remains unaffected by great distance and by physical barriers, according to experimental reports. Psi has apparently penetrated the ocean depths, soundproofing, cement, metal shielding, and even special electrified walls that are supposed to block both magnetic and radio waves. In fact, what psi seems to have the greatest difficulty penetrating is the conscious mind.

9.
The How and Why of Psi

While answers are beginning to be found to the who, what, where, and when of psi, the two most fundamental questions about the phenomenon remain unsolved. So far, no one knows how psi works, or why. As an experimental psychologist at the University of Edinburgh, John Beloff, wrote, ". . . though there has never been any lack of theorizing in this field, there is no theory that we could call an agreed theory."[1] Gardner Murphy says, "We have . . . no theoretical system tightly and beautifully organized in the manner of the architect."[2]

Even so, researchers speculate about the how and why of psi, drawn by the momentous questions its existence inevitably raises. Margaret Mead asks, "Does precognition add up to greater freedom of the will, or a new prescription for despair?"[3] And J. B. Rhine, who dropped his preministerial studies when he discovered that there was no accepted scientific basis for the existence of free will, urges that the research be pressed forward to find out whether people are more than just mechanical systems. He believes that the kinds of possible psychic ability that are currently being studied in parapsychology may yield evidence that another, transcendent side of human nature exists. He says, "It does not seem likely that human society, as we know and appreciate it, could exist without some firm awareness and understanding of this extraphysical side of human personality."[4]

In tentative response to these questions, some researchers postulate that psi may be some kind of communications link, without beginning and without ending, flowing between individuals and their environment.[5] Others say that psi, like peripheral vision, is always there, but it disappears when one looks at it. This was the comment of one potential young researcher who decided to become a psychiatrist instead of a parapsychologist.

William Braud and Lendell Braud speculate that psi may be a vestigial aspect of a survival mechanism to protect primitive people from predators.[6] Psychiatrist Jule Eisenbud uses this theory to explain why psi information is so faint. He says that if any one species had more psi than other species, that first species would be able to annihilate the others and so upset the ecological balance.[7]

Gardner Murphy speculates: "There may be forms of information systems which are not dependent upon the known sensory systems. It may be that there are senses whose receptor organs have not yet been discovered."[8] But J. B. Rhine disagrees, saying, "In spite of all efforts to link ESP with the world of physical processes, which science understands so relatively thoroughly, there appears to be no known physical condition or process to which it can be related."[9] And the Czechoslovakian observer Milan Ryzl argues that it is too soon to build theoretical constructions, pointing out that "the main questions about ESP and PK still remain to be answered."[10]

Certainly much more remains to be discovered than is so far known with certainty. But the early data which have been compiled make the search for more facts appear highly worthwhile. As has been shown, research findings indicate that nearly everyone can sometimes use psi to interact with nearly anything, at any distance, at any point in time. People seem to have little or no conscious control over psi. At this stage researchers do not know if it really can be controlled, or even if it should be controlled. But they do know it is there, just as Franklin knew the lightning was there. And just as the bright play of electricity in Franklin's garden presaged one of humanity's more important servants, so, too, psi may one day greatly affect the quality of human life. The possibilities are intriguing, the challenge enormous, and the rewards may be profound.

III.
Search

Not enough is known about psi or the processes by which it operates to say for certain what role it plays in human lives. What seems like psi may not be psi at all—and what does not seem like psi may be.

Inevitably, researchers must study psi in real life situations. As they move beyond the laboratory to the world at large, though the excitement may grow, the precision diminishes.

All around the concept of psi lies a thicket of unproved claims—from automatic writing to metal bending, from hauntings to auras to psi in plants. The explorer, if wise, will walk with extreme care, but with eyes open to the mysteries of the universe.

10.
Psi Beyond
Laboratory Walls

When psi investigation leaves the laboratory, researchers' problems multiply exponentially. Their carefully worked out laboratory controls against fraud vanish, and new, makeshift ones have to be created on the spot to match each specific situation being examined. Life swirls on around them, and the world's business continues as usual. When they study apparent spontaneous occurrences, researchers have no opportunity to screen subjects or randomize targets. They must investigate things as they happen, no matter what the circumstances. Sometimes it seems almost as if researchers are trying to keep leaves off the grass in the middle of a hurricane.

To get a better understanding of the difficulties of field research, it may be helpful to look at one example in detail. It involves some mysterious occurrences that attracted the attention of two psi researchers.

The Poltergeist in Mr. Laubheim's Warehouse
Around the middle of December 1966, Alvin Laubheim, manager and part-owner of Miami-based Tropication Arts, a wholesale distributor of Florida novelty items, noticed a sharp rise in warehouse breakage. The firm employed two shipping clerks—Curt Hagemayer, an older man, and Julio Vasquez, a nineteen-year-old Cuban refugee—and Laubheim assumed they were getting careless in stocking the glass and china items on the warehouse shelves.

Despite his admonitions to the clerks to be more careful, the breakage continued. On January 12, Laubheim went into the warehouse to personally demonstrate storage procedures, intending to put a halt to the losses. Breakage among the glass beer mugs was particularly high, so Laubheim took extra trouble to arrange the glasses properly himself. He put them, handles down, well at the back of the shelf where they were normally stored. Instructing the two clerks to look closely at what he had done, Laubheim said that if they stored the glasses that way they would avoid further breakage. No sooner had he walked to the end of the tier of storage shelves than a beer mug crashed to the floor behind him. He whirled at once and saw that both employees were at least fifteen feet away from the shelves. How had the beer mug managed to move across eight inches of shelf to fall to the floor?

By January 14 the breakage had become so serious that

Some of the breakage in Mr. Laubheim's warehouse.

Laubheim, at his partner's urging, reported it to the police. When they heard his strange story of a mysterious ghost that persisted in throwing glasses off shelves, their first reaction was that he must be mad. But soon after Patrolman William Killin arrived at the warehouse in response to Laubheim's complaint, he saw a glass fall to the floor and break. Two other patrolmen and a sergeant were called in. All four police officers were present when a box of address books, stored six to eight inches from the edge of a shelf, tumbled into the aisle.

From that point, events moved swiftly. Insurance investigators, TV crews, reporters, writers, and even a magician investigated the case. Perhaps most important of all, two distinguished parapsychologists, W.G. Roll and J. Gaither Pratt, became involved.

Both men have written extensively about what they observed. Some of the articles have appeared in the journals.[1] In addition to writing several scientific articles on the subject, Roll has also included a lengthy analysis of the case in his popular book *The Poltergeist*.[2] Pratt has written on the same case in collaboration with Roll and in one of his own works.[3]

The parapsychologists hypothesized that they were witnessing a fairly rare phenomenon called a *poltergeist* (from the German for noisy ghost). Over the period of the disturbances, they investigated a total of 224 mysterious breakages, some of which happened before they came to Miami and some after they arrived.

Investigators and employees alike soon noted that the mysterious breakages took place when and only when young Vasquez was in the warehouse. The scientists, wary of possible trickery, devised numerous elaborate schemes to determine whether or not Vasquez was indulging in a massive hoax. Areas were cordoned off and special monitoring systems were employed.

The result? No one ever detected any evidence of trickery, surreptitious pushing or throwing, or any other indication of fraud, either conscious or unconscious, on the part of Vasquez or any other person connected with the case. However, neither parapsychologist himself ever saw an object actually start from a resting position and sail through the air to the floor.

The nearest the parapsychologists came to actually witnessing any extraordinary movement of an object was on Saturday, January 28. The two scientists were standing four feet away from Vasquez, the older shipping clerk was at a wrapping desk to the rear, and all four men were talking about the poltergeist events. No one else was in the warehouse. They suddenly heard the sound of breaking glass in an aisle behind Vasquez and found a tall glass in pieces on the floor. Although they had not seen the glass move, they were convinced that it was impossible for the glass to have fallen by any ordinary means.

Several nonscientists claimed to have seen objects move in the warehouse. On one occasion two people, watching from different vantage points, both said they saw something move. Mrs. Joyce M. George, sister of Laubheim, and Mrs. Ruth May, one of the employees who decorated the souvenir pieces, both described the fall of an Orange Crush bottle. George told another visitor to the warehouse that she saw the bottle leave the shelf where it was stored, go "way out in the air, then down with a bang on its neck. Then it bounced on its side three times."[4]

One of the most fascinating aspects of the case was the personality of Julio Vasquez, the person with whom all these events were associated. Vasquez did not like one of the men for whom he worked in the warehouse. He once remarked to a researcher when his employer was berating another employee, "That's no way to talk to a man." The scientists believe that although Vasquez came in for his share of such treatment, he may have felt unable to fight back because he wanted to keep his job.

The outcome of the case was unfortunate. Vasquez was laid off from his job on February 1, partly because of the virtually complete halt brought to the regular warehouse activities by the distracting presence of the poltergeist and partly because he was under suspicion as the burglar who had broken into the warehouse a few days before. At the invitation of the parapsychologist Roll, he went to Durham, North Carolina, for extensive testing—during which time "his" poltergeist allegedly broke a vase in the lab of J. B. Rhine (the only supposed poltergeist occurrence in a parapsychology laboratory to date). Roll offered to send him to school for training in electronics, but Vasquez declined and returned to Miami. Poltergeist disturbances occurred at the various other places where he found employment. When last heard from, he was in prison in Puerto Rico. Roll does not know what charge brought him there.

Looking back on the strange series of events, Pratt says, "I have no doubt in my mind that it was a genuine case. There's no room

Julio Vasquez, warehouse shipping clerk, always present when the mysterious breakages occurred.

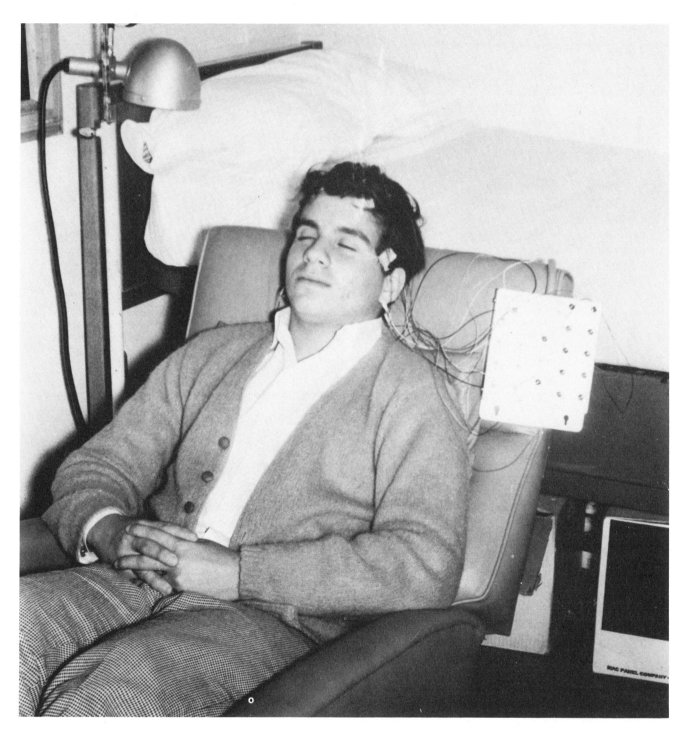

Julio Vasquez undergoing testing in a parapsychology laboratory.

for doubt in view of the circumstances under which we were able to make our own observations.''[5]

Vasquez's case seemed, in the minds of both these scientists, to fit the pattern of numerous collected reports of similar happenings. Probably the first poltergeist case on record is listed on an Egyptian papyrus. Jacob Grimm, in his *Deutsche Mythologie* (1835) describes a case reported around A.D. 355 involving a house in which stones were thrown about, blows issued from the walls, and people were yanked from their beds.

Early observers of poltergeist phenomena believed that the devil was behind these mysterious occurrences. In 1716-1717 a poltergeist erupted in the house of Samuel Wesley, father of John Wesley, who eventually founded the Methodist Church. The Wesley family concluded that a demon was at the root of the problem.[6]

Later, researchers came to hypothesize that the living, not the dead, caused poltergeist occurrences through PK. Among the first people to make this connection were two Swedish researchers, Hjalmar Wijk and Paul Bjerre. In a 1905 reported Swedish poltergeist case they hypnotized a woman with whom the events appeared to be connected. Apparently as a result of the hypnosis, the poltergeist events ceased.[7]

Typically, poltergeist occurrences are associated with adolescents or people whose emotions may be quite unstable. Usually some element of powerful but repressed anger is present. Psychological tests of Julio Vasquez showed he had feelings of impetuousness, frustration, and rage. In addition, he had openly expressed his indignation over the tactics of the warehouse boss.

When researchers study a poltergeist case in real life, such as the Vasquez case, they have to examine all possible explanations and causes for the events. Just because an object moves or breaks under mysterious circumstances, one cannot conclude that some psi force is at work.

Researchers first have to be sure that the reported events really are taking place and are not simply due to the imagination (or even deliberate hoaxing) of the people involved in them. Often investigation will reveal that the mysterious movements and breaking objects are the result of a practical joke by people in the family or the office. If no joke is involved, then the investigator must decide if the mysterious occurrence could be caused by chance, or be a misinterpretation of normal physical events. Many "poltergeists" turn out to be creakings and crackings in a house that is settling or sounds caused by sonic booms from supersonic aircraft. Squirrels in the attic have been known to produce strange noises at night, and the midnight creaks of a house may become spirit footsteps to a suddenly awakened sleeper. Sometimes several different explanations seem to be present in any one case.

After ordinary possibilities have been eliminated, investigators attempt to reconstruct the sequence of unexplained events, with accurate descriptions and analysis of sound, movements, and other effects. They attempt to interview all the individuals involved and chart their locations and what they report seeing. When funds and space permit, researchers set up equipment on the scene for observations and recording via video monitoring, sound recording, and other instruments. Hans Bender of the University of Freiburg, West Germany, and one of the best known authorities on poltergeists in the world, is beginning to use equipment such as this quite extensively. In a few rare cases unexplained physical movements have been recorded on film.[8]

Poltergeist activity may be a form of unconscious PK. Because the PK apparently occurs spontaneously—without the person's consciously willing it—and because it may occur repeatedly, it has come to be referred to as *recurring spontaneous psychokinesis* (RSPK). Roll found RSPK a useful term to describe the events involving Vasquez, and has written that, in his judgment, "The Miami disturbances can most reasonably be interpreted as a case of RSPK."[9] Through this explanation, Roll is offering a possible connection between a property of psi demonstrated in the laboratory—PK—and a strange phenomenon observed in the field. If people can affect the fall of dice, perhaps on occasion a few minds may be able, without their conscious knowledge, to whirl heavy objects from shelves to the floor.

The Miami incidents will probably never be wholly resolved, but they cannot be ignored. It may well be that from a study of what are presently unexplained occurrences researchers will gain valuable insights into psi's workings. One must remember, however, that it is tremendously difficult to decide what may be psi and what may not be.

In the three chapters that follow, a number of unexplained occurrences will be examined. In each case, four questions must be asked: Did this really happen? If it did, is there a way to explain what happened in ordinary, non-psi terms? If there is not, is it psi-related? If so, how?

The subjects that follow have been associated with or attributed to psi by many. They have not been studied extensively in the laboratory. Many are controversial; many, upon analysis, appear to have no relation to psi at all. These are topics about which there is rarely any agreement even among researchers.

11.
Some Traditional Associations

A number of phenomena involving alleged unusual human abilities have traditionally been associated with psi.* These include Spiritualism, mediums, apparations and hauntings, automatisms, levitation, reincarnation, auras, and some occult systems of divination. Many of these beliefs began as fads, or as religious doctrines, and were able to attract numerous followers because of their strong emotional impact.

Spiritualism
The most widespread practice of the nineteenth century involving alleged psychic abilities was called Spiritualism. It originated in England in 1848 when two teenaged sisters named Fox claimed that they could communicate with the spirit of a dead man, a peddler who had been murdered. He rapped on the walls of the house where they lived, they explained, and they had managed to decipher the code underlying the raps. Joined by a third sister, the Fox girls traveled around the world. They sat around tables from which emanated mysterious raps, and which sometimes even appeared to rise off the floor. The sisters were tested by several commissions of scientists and journalists; their reports were contradictory. Later, two of the sisters said their spiritualist claims were fraudulent. Nonetheless, Spiritualism swept much of the western world for a time, and a few Spiritualist societies continue in the 1970s.

Both believers and skeptics pressed for a deeper understanding of the Fox sisters' powers and those of others who soon came on the scene. Much to the dismay of the public, psychical investigators uncovered numerous instances of charlatanism, elaborate hoaxes, and fraud. Henry Slade, who boasted the ability to cause writing to magically appear on sealed slates, was exposed by a professor in England, Edwin Lankester, who explained how Slade prepared the writing beforehand. An 1887 report by The Seybert Commission, appointed by the University of Pennsylvania "to Investigate Modern Spiritualism," blasted the claims it had examined.[1] And even some of those who had alleged they possessed psychic ability joined in producing exposés. Several

The Fox Sisters (in 1848), who claimed they could communicate with the dead.

*In considering the multitudinous case histories, reports, field studies, and laboratory investigations available, the authors have endeavored to choose representative instances. The information in this chapter and the two that follow is not to be considered a comprehensive review of all the existing material, but simply an overview of what has been done in these areas.

wrote confessions explaining the devious ways in which they had produced their wondrous results.

The public, indignant at the reports of fakery, moved on to other interests. The general disgust was so great that it stigmatized not only spiritualists but also those who uncovered fraudulent practices.[2] Even today in the minds of many people, psychic researchers are inherently suspect.[3]

Early Research Into Psychic Anecdotes

Although public attention shifted from mediums to other matters, psychical researchers persisted. Their societies provided collection places for numerous reports of apparent spontaneous psi—reports that continue to the present day. Researchers soon realized that these reports were almost valueless in their raw form. They undertook to present and analyze them systematically. "Our job in psychical research," Gardner Murphy wrote as late as 1953, "consists in having a plan with reference to the gathering of spontaneous cases—a systematic, careful interpretation . . . and then testing our hypothesis against fresh facts. . . ."[4] He added, "There is a definite place in science for the systematic arrangements of events which are not under experimental control."[5]

Researchers today disagree as to the reliability of the early reports. One investigator who takes a dim view of them described ". . . the difficulty of deciding what allowance should be made for normal possibilities, such as chance coincidence and unconscious exaggeration. . . . the report is based upon the testimony of unskilled observers who are often emotionally implicated in the phenomena they describe. In such circumstances it is extremely difficult to form a balanced judgment."[6]

Fairly typical of the kind of report to which the investigator is referring is a July 1895 report by one Martyn Smith, published in the *Journal of the Society for Psychical Research*. Described by the author as "clearly a case of thought-transference,"[7] the report concerned the dream of an Englishwoman named Mrs. Jeffries that allegedly helped the police locate the body of her missing niece. Smith first learned of this case through a newspaper account of the subsequent inquest into the niece's death.

Smith interviewed Jeffries and described her version of the events as follows. Her niece, thirteen-year-old Rose Foster, had been staying with her for some weeks. On Wednesday, April 17, 1895, Jeffries and her niece quarreled. Afterward, Rose left the house and did not return. On Thursday, Rose's brother visited Jeffries saying he was worried about his sister and feared she might have killed herself. Although Jeffries pooh-poohed the idea, that night she had a disturbing dream. Smith writes, "She thought she was walking along the side of the canal at Spring Hill with an umbrella, which she let touch to ripple the water; when at a certain spot she saw the face of her niece appear above the surface twice, and the second time she caught it by the hair, lifted her out and clasped her to her breast and kissed her. She woke up after the dream, much terrified."[8]

The next day, Friday, Jeffries heard that the police had been told her niece was missing and were dragging the Spring Hill

Early Investigative Groups

The most important early group formed to investigate mediums was the Society for Psychical Research (SPR), formed in London in 1882. Its founders included classical scholars and philosophers from Cambridge University and physicists. Among its leaders were some of the most illustrious thinkers of the day. Scholars and Spiritualists cooperated in guiding the SPR.

After a leader of the SPR visited the United States, several interested American scientists formed the American Society for Psychical Research (ASPR). One of its most distinguished early members was the philosopher William James. Both societies are still in existence today.

canal in a search for her body. She went at once to the water's edge, where she met her niece's brother and also Acting Inspector Whittingham, who, with two other police officers, was engaged in the dragging operations. As Whittingham later testified at the inquest, Jeffries told him that she had dreamed the night before of her niece and had clearly seen her drowning in the canal, but at a spot some fifty-five to sixty yards away from where they were presently dragging. Since they had not found the body where they were, Whittingham agreed to try the spot Jeffries indicated. There, just as she predicted, they found the body. When it was discovered, Smith wrote, "The face of the girl appeared above the water, just as she (Mrs. Jeffries) had seen it (in sleep); it sank again, the second time the face appeared in the same position, and the brother leaped into the water and clasped the body to his breast and kissed the face as the aunt had dreamt she herself had done."[9]

Although the aunt claimed a premonitory dream, a number of alternative explanations are possible. She could have actually known of the body's location in a number of other ways: she could have spotted a pale face under the water, perhaps, or she could even have killed her niece herself and disposed of the body in the place she later indicated to the police. Even if her story was the exact truth, the incident could have been one of simple coincidence.

Indeed, a search of the literature of the early years of psi research yields disappointing results. A member of the Society for Psychical Research, Hilda Harding, an English barrister who claimed to have had psychic dreams and impressions herself, reviewed a cross-section of fifteen volumes of reported cases from 1884 to the late 1940s, and concluded that the evidence had "little value for the unbiased examiner, hardly anything emerging which could be called first class."[10]

The librarian of the Parapsychology Foundation, a private foundation founded by the well-known medium Eileen Garrett, recently wrote the authors in response to a request for help on this subject: "After quite extensive literature search, and speaking with several people who know the literature, I found out that there were always extremely few good cases of spontaneous phenomena, and as for more recent cases, apparently none reported in the literature withstand a closer scrutiny."[11] D. J. West states, ". . . the perfect case is a myth. There is always a flaw somewhere, either in the circumstances of the experience or in the supporting evidence."[12]

Apparitions and Hauntings
The kinds of things early psychical researchers investigated formed a wide range of difficult-to-explain phenomena. Again and again these scientists attempted to devise effective, systematic ways to investigate the various incidents, but even their best efforts inevitably ended in ambiguity.[13]

One category that received much attention involved apparitions and hauntings. An apparition is an image that suggests the real presence of a person who is actually very far away or is dead. A haunting is alleged to be the manifestation of the presence of a dead person in a particular place. Reports of such phenomena received widespread research interest among psychical researchers because they appeared to offer the possibility of confirming that life continues after death.

An early account of a haunting comes from the ancient Roman philosopher Athenodorus, who said he was plagued by a ghost that rattled chairs at him. The philosopher said he followed the figure to a courtyard, where it vanished. Upon digging up the earth in the spot where the ghost had vanished, Athenodorus uncovered the remains of a skeleton in chains.[14]

Early psychical investigators reported the case of a Russian woman who claimed to see "a large grey shadow," which resembled an Army colonel whose death was announced the following day.[15] A Reverend Tweedale described the simultaneous apparition of his grandmother to himself and to his father. The day after the apparition, news of her death was telegraphed to the family.[16] The *Journal of the American Society for Psychical Research* carried the report of a former Polish Army Officer concerning an apparition that correctly foretold disaster. The night it was seen, the house in which it appeared was burned to the ground.[17]

The Cheltenham haunting, one of the best known haunted house stories, was reported by Rosina Despard, a medical student whose reports, although uncorroborated, were taken quite seriously by contemporary investigators. She described seeing on numerous occasions the figure of a rather tall woman with a handkerchief held up to her face. In an attempt at careful investigation, Despard placed threads across a stairway where the figure had sometimes appeared and later saw the ghost move through the strings. An investigation of the history of the house revealed that a woman had died there as a result of chronic alcoholism. Despard said that woman, as described to her, matched the figure she had seen.[18] In more recent times Gertrude Schmeidler has attempted two separate quantitative investigations of haunted houses. Schmeidler's results, in her opinion, did indicate that something was taking place, but did not reveal anything about the phenomena.[19+, 20+] *

Possible explanations for apparitions and hauntings vary. Early researchers thought they might either be spirits of the dead or else caused by them. However, in over a century of investigation, no one has yet come up with any concrete proof that they, in fact, an indication of life after death. G. N. M. Tyrrell argued that apparitions are physically created nonphysical hallucinations, built up between the unconscious minds of those who see the apparition and the person who is projecting it.[21] As for hauntings, some researchers speculate that violent emotions may impress themselves on the atmosphere of a house. According to this theory, later residents of the house may then act like motion picture projectors, allowing these violent scenes to be replayed.

*In an effort to avoid deluging the reader with experimental details in this SEARCH section, the authors simply report experimental highlights. When a note number has a + next to it, the note contains not only the experimental reference but also additional information on the experiment itself or on related experiments.

Automatism

In addition to unusual occurrences, such as apparitions and hauntings, early researchers also studied people who seemed to have unusual abilities. One such ability, automatism, is manifested when an individual performs actions that are allegedly not controlled by his conscious mind. Automatisms have been reported in such forms as automatic writing, automatic painting, and automatic musical composition. Early researchers focused on automatisms because they believed the automatisms provided objective evidence that some psychical event was taking place.

Automatisms flourished in the heyday of Spiritualism. Many Spiritualists maintained automatisms were caused by the spirits of the dead. Most mediums of the period practiced automatic writing and were joined by, among others, Harriet Beecher Stowe, who claimed that part of her *Uncle Tom's Cabin* had been written that way. In 1883 the Catholic mystic Ann Catherine Emmerich claimed to automatically write on the life of Christ, and her manuscripts were classed by the church as divinely inspired.[22]

Probably the most famous automatism was that displayed by Pearl Lenore Curran of St. Louis. By spelling out words one at a time on a Ouija board, Curran produced four full-length books, thousands of poems, countless epigrams and aphorisms, short stories, and even a few plays. She attributed all these words to Patience Worth, who allegedly had died many years before, and for whom she was acting, through the Ouija board, as the agent of transmission.

Several factors made Curran's claims noteworthy. She had gone only to grade school and had read little. Yet her automatisms displayed "... knowledge, genius and versatility of literary expression, philosophic depth, piercing wit, spirituality, and swiftness of thought."[23] Even her means of production was remarkable. One observer, Professor Otto Heller of Washington University, found himself baffled by the rapidity with which she worked at the Ouija board. "... on its mechanical side the performance was scarcely short of miraculous. To realize that, spell out aloud consecutively some printed pages at a steady rate of about 36 words a minute. Unless you, too, have your connection with some invisible prompter, I predict that in less than five minutes you will be fumbling and stumbling with all of your letters."[24]

The major researchers of the day investigated Pearl Lenore Curran extensively and were unable to uncover any evidence of fraud. They noted that her father had been a professional writer, but he had never encouraged her attempts at ordinary writing as a child. Possibly she had developed her automatic writing talent as a way to write, which, because it was attributed to "Patience Worth," was not strictly hers and thus not a threat to her father's position as the head of the family and the "official" writer. Psychical researcher Walter Franklin concluded, "Either our concept of what we call the subconscious must be radically altered, so as to include potencies of which we hitherto have had no knowledge, or else some cause operating through but not originating in the subconsciousness of Mrs. Curran must be acknowledged."[25]

Pearl Lenore Curran, whose automatic writings as Patience Worth attracted the attention of literary critics.

A Ouija board and pointer (planchette) in use.

Two explanations for automatic writing—other than that it comes from the dead—rely on the operations of the unconscious. Many psychologists believe that Ouija board movements and automatic writing are caused by minute muscle movements in the operator's own hands. The person's unconscious mind, they think, is actually spelling out the messages. A psi-oriented explanation postulates that the unconscious mind does this by gathering information through ESP. This would account for automatic writing that, upon investigation, is found to be correct but that contains information apparently unknown to the operator's conscious mind. Rather than communicating with the dead, this theory says, the operator gathers the information unconsciously through ESP and then communicates it through the automatic practice.

Levitation
An equally striking phenomenon allegedly observed on numerous occasions is levitation. An apparent violation of the law of gravity, levitation occurs when a person or object rises from the ground or other stable base by extraordinary means. A table lifts itself off the floor and remains suspended for a few seconds; a coffee cup moves slowly through the air and even turns a corner; a

human being suddenly floats two feet off the ground. These are the claims for levitation.

Today few reports of levitation are made, and no study of the phenomenon is currently under way in the United States. The sensitives Uri Geller and Nina Kulagina allegedly can levitate small objects, but such events have not been observed under controlled conditions.

In the past, however, reports of levitation were not so rare. Early Christian history is spotted with accounts of the levitation of the human body. Oliver LeRoy, in his book *Levitation*, lists some two hundred levitating saints. The saint who was best known for his alleged levitations was St. Joseph of Copertino (1603–1663). Credited with some seventy levitations, St. Joseph was observed by people as distinguished as Johann Friedrich, Duke of Brunswick, the patron of the philosopher Leibnitz. The Duke said that he saw

(Left) D. D. Home, the Scottish-American medium and alleged levitator. (Right) An artist's conception of Home levitating.

St. Joseph levitate while the saint was in the act of prayer. St. Theresa of Avila (1515–1582), one of the greatest saints of the period, was also reported by her convent sisters to have levitated.[26]

After the birth of Spiritualism, the levitation of objects and of the human body became a relatively common form of psychic phenomena. Perhaps the best known alleged levitations were those of the Scottish-American medium D. D. Home, who first reportedly levitated himself in 1852 and whose feats were witnessed by several scientists. Home, the most famous medium of his day, was never discovered in any fraudulent practices. One of the scientists who observed Home levitating was the Englishman William Crookes, later knighted for his achievements in chemistry. Crookes was known for his profound suspicion of alleged psychic phenomena. After a careful study of Home, however, Crookes reversed his position, saying his experiments and observations "appear conclusively to establish the existence of a new force."[27]

Some critics of psychic phenomena argue that levitation does not exist. They point out that epileptics and hysterics often arch their bodies during spasms. They suggest that these archings, in which only the head and feet touch the floor, might easily be misinterpreted by credulous witnesses as levitation.

Others disagree. Accepting that with PK humans possess a mind-over-matter ability, they believe that people may be able to use PK on themselves to levitate their own bodies. Some Soviet scientists are toying with the idea of antigravity. They speculate that human beings possess a force that does not necessarily lift them into the air but that nullifies the force of gravity, allowing the body (or an object) to float up into the air. They call this biogravitation.[28]

Mediums

One of the outgrowths of the Spiritualist period was the rise of mediums. Following in the footsteps of the table-rapping Fox sisters, mediums claimed to be able to communicate information received from unknown sources. Most mediums, but not all, claim their unknown sources are the dead, who they believe live on in the form of spirits, which they call discarnate entities. The name *medium* derives from the way these people allegedly obtain the information: they let the unknown source (known as a control) speak, write, or move through the medium of their body.

The soothsayers of ancient times were obviously the first mediums. During the Roman imperial age, according to the classical scholar E. R. Dodds, mediumship proper was practiced.[29] In addition to official oracles, the Greeks also relied upon people called belly-talkers. These were lay people who allegedly had spirits within them that spoke through them. Even Plato refers to these people in his writings.

The idea that people could communicate with the departed generated wide public interest when Emanuel Swedenborg (1688–1772), a Swedish genius and scientist, started to preach that he could make contact with the dead and bring forth messages from them. According to contemporary accounts, some of Swedenborg's demonstrations were remarkably impressive. Swedenborg's influence spread, and in 1844 in the United States, Andrew Jackson Davis, an illiterate (or so he claimed) New York country boy began preaching under spirit guidance. Other religious sects, such as the Shakers, also practiced mediumship.

When the Society for Psychical Research was founded in 1882, it soon discovered a medium named Leonore Piper, who would go into a trance and bring through messages apparently from the dead. Leaders of the S.P.R. studied her over several decades and many investigators, including the philosopher William James, came to the conclusion that she possessed psychic abilities. Some of them came to believe that she actually was in touch with the dead.[30+]

Eileen Garrett (1893–1970) was one of the most remarkable mediums of all time. Orphaned two weeks after her birth as a result of the double suicide of her parents, Garrett had a lonely and unhappy childhood. Yet during her early years she allegedly had companions whom no one else could see, talked to plants, had visions, and saw rays of light around her classmates.

Garrett's apparent abilities were developed under the direction

The famous medium Eileen J. Garrett, who sought unsuccessfully to discover the source of her unusual abilities.

of the British College of Psychic Science, and she became a medium. People came to her for help in locating missing persons or objects, for advice about their lives, and for many other purposes. Her success at these tasks was striking, and she attained a reputation as a person of unusual gifts.

Unlike most mediums, Garrett was not convinced that in her trances she was indeed bringing forth communications from the dead. She went to considerable lengths to try to uncover the source of her unusual abilities. Her daughter, Eileen Coly, says of her famous mother, "She was not only willing but eager to undergo scientific investigation in order to shed some light on this unusual ability which plagued her all her life. She sought professional persons of very high caliber. On the whole, she was not convinced of life after death. She wanted to learn about herself so she could try to get it straight for everyone."[31]

Garrett was investigated by most of the well-known researchers of the time, including J. B. Rhine, but the origin of her abilities was never uncovered. She asked the noted psychotherapist Ira Progoff to try to determine, on the basis of his studies in the field of depth psychology, the nature and meaning of the voices that spoke through her. Were they really discarnate beings? Or did they have some other meaning?

Progoff, after months of intensive examination of Garrett, could find no meaning or explanation. He said that Garrett explained "as she had reflected upon the events and situations of her life, she had progressively realized that a great many people around the world were basing their beliefs about the nature of immortality and their personal expectations for life after death upon the descriptions of certain experiences that had happened to her. But so far as she herself was concerned she could neither validate or disprove them."[32]

One of the more curious experiments to test Garrett involved a skeptical physician at Roosevelt Hospital in New York City. His physiological tests of Garrett (which were never published in a professional journal) yielded sharply different results, depending on whether she was awake, in a trance under a control being named Abdul, or in a trance under a control named Ouvani. For example, when she was in a normal waking state, her blood clotting time was about 180 seconds; as Ouvani, the time was 33 seconds; and for Abdul, 90 seconds or so. The physician, although greatly intrigued, was never able to find a satisfactory explanation for these differences. Later physiological tests by others (also unpublished) found no difference whether Garrett was awake or in a trance.[33] The Roosevelt test failed to be corroborated by any subsequent investigations.

Eileen Garrett is also remembered as the founder of the Parapsychology Foundation, which has fostered interdisciplinary dialogues between parapsychologists and scholars from other disciplines. From time to time, the foundation also supports many of the major psi researchers through grants.

Most psi researchers feel that at least some mediums have shown that they can gain extrasensory information, even though their statements contain, "besides correct data, many errors, inaccuracies, and symbolisms."[34] The debate is over the origin of that information. Some postulate that the medium telepathically taps the mind of the client. Others advance the super-ESP hypothesis, where the medium allegedly scans the living world via telepathy and clairvoyance to gain information that can then be passed off as coming from the dead. Yet others believe that the medium is, in fact, communicating either directly or indirectly with the dead and they take this as proof of survival after death.

Reincarnation

A major thread running throughout the pages of psychical history in both England and the United States is the interest of early researchers in the possibility of life after death, sometimes referred to as survival phenomena. Some of the theories advanced to explain automatic writing, apparitions, hauntings, mediumship, and other phenomena rested on a belief in life after death. Another manifestation of humanity's hunger for immortality is the belief that the spirit of a dead person can be born again in a new body through reincarnation. Despite all the investigative work done on the subject, however, no one has yet been able to produce conclusive evidence of life after death.

Plato accepted the idea of reincarnation and stated the case for it in his *Phaedo*. Pythagoras actively taught the doctrine. It was also taught in the Talmud, and a number of early Christian sects believed in reincarnation. But it is in Hindu and Buddhist thought that reincarnation holds fullest sway.[35]

An example of recent work done to investigate a reported case of reincarnation can be found in Ian Stevenson's investigation of an Indian man named Bishen Chand.[36] Although a number of similar cases have been reported in India, Stevenson feels the Chand case has one feature that makes it of particular interest. Chand first made statements that others interpreted to mean he remembered a past life at the age of $2\frac{1}{2}$ years. When he was $5\frac{1}{2}$, his statements were recorded by a lawyer, K. K. N. Sahay, who had heard of the case. These statements were recorded before any attempt was made to verify them. In most supposed reincarnation cases, by contrast, the person's statements are recorded only *after* some of them appear to have been verified. Such a sequence results in the possibility that the statements can be distorted— intentionally or unintentionally—to fit the known facts of the person's alleged previous life. This possibility does not exist in the Chand case.

Bishen Chand was born in 1921 to poor parents in Bareilly, Uttar Pradesh. Almost as soon as he began to talk, he began saying the word *Pilvit* or *Pilivit*. Pilibhit is the name of a town about fifty kilometers away from Bareilly where the Kapoor family had no relatives or any other associations. As Bishen Chand began to speak more, he described many details of a life he claimed he had lived in Pilibhit, said his father was a wealthy landowner and that his own name was Laxmi Narain, criticized his Kapoor father for the family's poverty, and complained, "Even my servant would not take the food cooked here."[37]

The lawyer Sahay took the child Chand to Pilibhit to check out his story. Chand allegedly recognized various places there and made additional statements about his supposedly previous life in

Pilibhit. The things Chand recognized and the statements he made corresponded closely in many instances to the facts of the life of a man named Laxmi Narain, who had died there a little more than two years before Chand's birth. Stevenson concludes that it is extremely unlikely that Chand "could have acquired by normal means all the information related to the previous life that he showed between the ages of two and a half and five and a half. He was five and a half when first taken to Pilibhit."[38]

One possible explanation for cases such as the Chand one is that these children are unconsciously using their ESP ability. Since they live in cultures that teach reincarnation, they may interpret this ESP information as the recollection of a previous life. Another, highly controversial, theory speculates that such a child has inherited from his ancestors memories of past ages and people, which are passed off as recollections of previous lives. Alternatively, some believe that the Chand story represents an instance of possession by a dead person.

Auras

Auras are alleged to be emanations that surround all living organisms, revealing information about the mental and physical state of the organisms. Some people claim to be able to see auras.

References to auras are found throughout metaphysical literature. Countless religious pictures, particularly those of Christ and Buddha, feature halos, which some consider to be representative of auras.

Suggestions for studying auras have been made by Charles Tart,[39] and some pilot attempts at studying them have been described by A.R.G. Owen of the New Horizons Research Foundation. But at the present time there is no scientific evidence to show that the aura exists. Impressions of the aura may be psychic in nature, or a psychological projection on the part of the aura reader, or something representing one of the known physical fields, such as light or heat, that surround the human body.

Shafica Karagulla, a Los Angeles neuropsychiatrist with a background of research and practice in four countries, has worked with many sensitives who describe interpenetrating fields of energy around the human being—the vital, the emotional, and the mental. To the sensitives these alleged fields are clearly discernible. They say they are able to observe an effect on any one field at any one time, and they report that certain activities, ideas, or experiences seem to increase the flow of energy into a specific field. However, the energy fields and patterns the sensitives claim to see have not yet been verified by instrumentation.[40] Nor has Karagulla published any of her results in the scientific journals.

Astrology, I Ching, Tarot Cards, and Palmistry

Because precognition is one of the major forms of psi, some people assume that occult systems of divination are also related to psi. These include astrology, the I Ching, Tarot cards, and palmistry.

Astrology, bolstered by columns in daily newspapers, magazines, and paperback books, has a large popular following today. Astrologers maintain that people and events are affected by the position of the planets, the sun, and other heavenly bodies. Astrologers have been consulted throughout recorded history by people as diverse as the ancient Egyptians and Adolf Hitler. But there have been no scientific studies published implying any relationship between astrology and psi. Nor have there been any such studies on astrology as a divining technique.

The small numbers of studies published to determine the predictive value of astrology have been mainly negative in their results. Michel Gauquelin made 7,482 comparisons of astrological signs with personality and vocational traits, concluding that the results showed only a random distribution of successful match-ups.[41]

The *I Ching*—the ancient Chinese *Book of Changes*—and Tarot cards are both used by various people to attempt to predict an individual's future and to determine personal actions. Lawrence Rubin and Charles Honorton attempted to relate psi to *I Ching* in their experiment "Separating the Yins from the Yangs."[42] They found that those subjects who believed in the possible existence of psi obtained answers pertaining to their particular problems from the *I Ching* at statistically more significant levels than did those who were skeptical about psi. No study to establish a connection between psi and Tarot cards has been attempted.

Based on the supposition that a person's palm reveals information about that individual's past, present, and future, palmistry as a form of divination dates back at least to the Vedic writings of

Some cards from a Tarot deck.

India some three thousand years ago. As far as is known, there is no scientific verification for the claims of palmists, and no studies to link palmistry with psi.

There is no evidence that any of these systems of divination are based on psi. In operation, however, they allow considerable latitude for the practitioner's interpretive judgment and intuitive impression, as do crystal balls and tea leaves. J. B. Rhine has pointed out that such interpretation could make use of the psi ability of the practitioner.[43] However, this possibility has not been tested under controlled conditions.

Topics such as Spiritualism and reincarnation are difficult to deal with scientifically. Events associated with them can be explained in many ways; it is almost impossible to conduct any controlled experiments to discover what psychological, physical, or psi factors might be involved. Consequently, these topics are often turned into belief systems to be taken on faith or denied.

In an attempt to avoid this complex problem, and also to escape the emotional biases associated with these topics, most psychical researchers turned to laboratory research, where less spectacular but more solid results could be obtained. The four cornerstones of psi were postulated and identified in laboratory work, and these have been the focus of the scientific study of the field. Ironically, the research on telepathy, clairvoyance, precognition, and psychokinesis may now be clarifying such theories and concepts as Spiritualism, reincarnation, and the spontaneous psychic events that baffled early investigators.

12.
Some New Interests

While such phenomena as levitation, mediumship, and reincarnation are less in vogue than they used to be, some new phenomena have come to the attention of the public. Scientists in a number of disciplines have been excited by the development of biofeedback techniques. The Kirlian effect, the possibility of psi in plants, and the question of metal bending have generated considerable controversy. Yet the verdict on all of these subjects of current interest is the same as that on those of the early days of psychical research—inconclusive. Scientists continue to ask: If this does occur, is it psi-related? And if it does occur and is not psi, then what is it?

Biofeedback

Among today's new interests are devices and techniques that some think might be of help in testing and eliciting psi. One technique several researchers view as promising is biofeedback. Using a variety of technologically sophisticated devices, biofeedback experts can help people become aware of a number of different unconscious mental or physical functions, such as blood pressure, heartbeat, skin temperature, and brain waves. Through this awareness, or *feedback,* with visual or auditory signals to indicate success, in many instances individuals can learn to control these functions consciously.

The connection between biofeedback and psi is only just now being made. "There is some hope that biofeedback can be used to bring at least some psychic ability under voluntary control. If this becomes a reality, it will likely be the most explosive, far-reaching discovery that biofeedback can make."[1] so comments Dr. Barbara Brown, a leading biofeedback researcher. Dr. Thomas Budzynski of the University of Colorado Medical School concurs: "When, through the rapidly advancing technology of bioelectronics, we can reliably define those biological response patterns that facilitate psi phenomena, biofeedback will be used to develop and sustain such patterns. Research of this sort is already underway and the preliminary results are very encouraging."[2] both Brown and Budzynski are biofeedback scientists, not psi scientists. Their interest in biofeedback's possible usefulness as a tool to enhance psi functioning is viewed by psi researchers as an example of the need for further interdisciplinary study of psi.

Results of biofeedback investigation have made it possible to explain phenomena that were previously considered paranormal. For many years scientists viewed the ability of certain Yogis

Biofeedback experts.

Barbara Brown of the Veterans Administration Hospital, Sepulveda, California.

Thomas Budzynski of the University of Colorado Medical School.

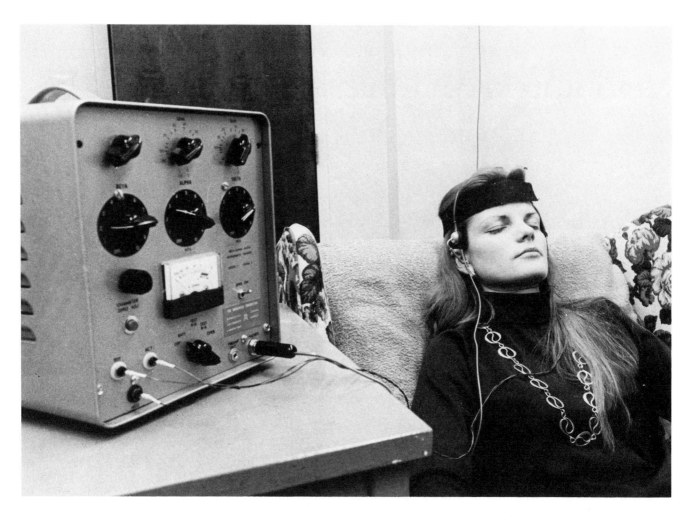

A Menninger Foundation researcher conducting biofeedback training.

and other contemplatives to regulate such physiological processes as their temperature, heartbeat, or brain-wave patterns as extraordinary. Such procedures were considered involuntary, not subject to conscious control. Now biofeedback has demonstrated that many physiological functions can in fact be brought under voluntary control, not only by Yogis but by quite ordinary people.

Kirlian Photography

In recent years a process known as Kirlian photography has become associated with psychic phenomena. A widespread and mistaken popular belief is that this technique produces a picture of the so-called *aura* or "psychic body." However, most parapsychologists, including J. B. Rhine, do not think that Kirlian photography is relevant to psi research,[3] and there is no conclusive scientific evidence that it is.

Kirlian photography is an outgrowth of a technique known in the West for many decades, called corona discharge photography, which is used mainly to identify flaws in metal used in engineering. Systematic study of the possible use of this diagnostic technique with human subjects was initiated by Semyon Davidovich Kirlian, a Soviet electrician. Kirlian claimed corona discharge photography could produce information from artificially produced fields around parts of living systems, such as leaves, hands,

A Kirlian photograph of a torn leaf.

and fingers. His first scientific report on this procedure appeared in the *Journal of Scientific and Applied Photography* in 1961.[4]*

The typical Kirlian device is a flat metal plate with unexposed film positioned on top of it. An object is placed on the film, and high voltage electricity, at very low amperage, is pulsed through the metal plate. The electricity passes through the film and exposes it. When developed, the film shows an outline of the object placed on the plate and also a halo of light surrounding the object. If the film is color sensitive, the corona discharge halo appears to have many colors.[5]

Thelma Moss has worked with these corona effects since 1970. Moss and her associates at UCLA have taken thousands of Kirlian photographs of people's fingertips and are convinced that changes that can be observed in such photographs reveal the emotional and physiological state of the person being photographed. So far the Moss team has been examining gross effects. None of their findings on how the Kirlian effect may relate to humans have been published in the scientific journals.

However, in a recent issue of *Psychoenergetic Systems*, Moss

*Because there is such a variety of opinions currently held about Kirlian photography, the authors have specified in the text which reports about the phenomenon were published in scientific journals and which were not.

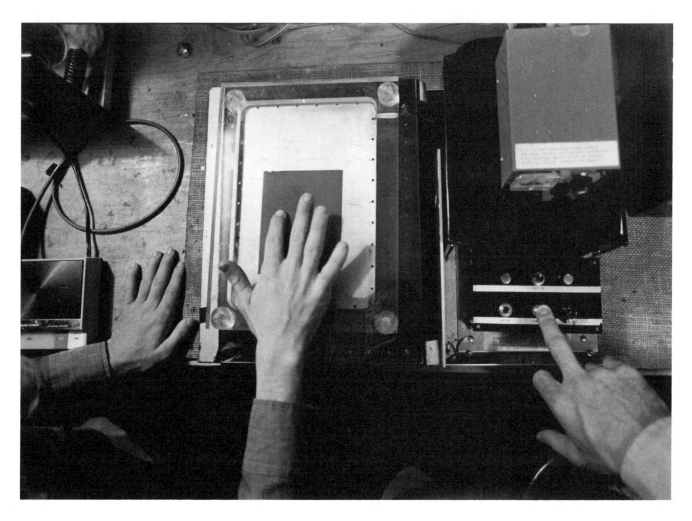

Kirlian photographic apparatus used to create an electrical field around a portion of the body placed on a photographic plate.

did report a study done with plant material, in which she claimed to have reproduced the Soviet's "phantom leaf" effect.[6] In this effect, after a portion of a leaf is removed and the remaining portion photographed, its Kirlian image still shows the original, intact leaf.

William A. Tiller, Professor of Materials Science at Stanford University, has reported on research into corona discharge photography in the *Journal of Applied Physics* and *New Scientist.*[7] He takes the view that:

> . . .we should not be at all surprised (or dismayed) to find a perfectly reasonable physical explanation for the generation of light and for the colour observations. The important and difficult step is to prove that such observations are indeed directly correlated with energy changes in the living system, rather than just the random fluctuations associated with inadequate experimental techniques. This has not yet been proved one way or the other.[8]

A drexel University research team, funded by the Advanced Research Project Agency of the Department of Defense, indicated in a recent report published in *Science* that there are at least twenty-five variables that need to be controlled in order to take proper Kirlian photographs.[9] These variables may cause some or all of the changes in Kirlian photographs. According to the Drexel team, it is impossible to compare *any* corona discharge photographs if all the variables are not known. (They regard the use of film as the source of a number of the more important and frustrating variables for the researcher. Their work is now moving towards using electro-optic equipment, which permits direct visual observation of the corona, to replace the film.)

Douglas Dean of the Newark College of Engineering has used Kirlian photography to study the hands of psychic healers.[10] He claims that when these individuals are attempting to heal others, their Kirlian images are larger and more vivid. Dean's observations are similar to the gross effects described by Moss. An attempt to replicate Dean's experiment was made by Frances Smith, but was not successful. The Dean study was not published in a scientific journal; the Smith study appeared in *The Journal of the American Society for Psychical Research.*[11]

If the corona discharge can be explained by known principles in electronics, then it is not a manifestation of psi.[12] Like other technical procedures, however, corona discharge photography may be used someday to study psi phenomena.[13] Meanwhile, physiological factors, such as sweat, finger pressure, and many other conditions, may explain most or all of the effects that result in Kirlian photography. Or perhaps the corona discharge halo can be influenced at a distance through psychokinesis. Alternatively, the corona discharges of experimental subjects may change as psi is manifested. Until more information is available, no final conclusions can be drawn.

Plants and Psi

A claim that recently stirred much public interest was the allegation by Cleve Backster that plants exhibit psi abilities. Several other researchers have attempted to replicate Backster's work. At this point the published research of other investigators does not offer laboratory evidence to substantiate his controversial claim.

Backster is by no means the first to postulate that plants may have some special attributes. Aristotle may be the first person in history to claim that plants have souls. The Jains, an Indian sect, will only eat grain, for they, too, believe that plants have souls. Professor Jagadish Chandra Bose of Calcutta's Presidency College, working around the beginning of the twentieth century, came to believe that plants possessed a life force. His work convinced him that plants responded to weak electric currents, just as humans do.[14]

Backster, a professional lie-detector examiner, reports that his involvement in plants was precipitated when he hooked up a galvanometer to a house plant in his New York office. He allegedly learned that the plant showed a reaction on the galvanometer not only to fire but also to his *plan* to set a leaf on fire.

Backster conducted a laboratory study to test the hypothesis that plants would respond to the death of brine shrimp.[15] Three philodendrons were wired to galvanometers on six occasions to see if their leaves would respond to the exact moment brine shrimp were killed by being dumped into boiling water. According to the three experts who analyzed the results, the galvanometer readouts showed a significantly higher electrical resistance on

Cleve Backster monitoring a plant.

the leaves on the single occasion when the shrimp were being killed than in the other time periods measured.

Backster's results caused great excitement among researchers, but later attempts to confirm them have failed. At Cornell, K. A. Horowitz, D. C. Lewis, and E. L. Gasteiger attempted to replicate Backster's work, and they were unable to do so.[16] Nor could R. V. Johnson of the University of Washington.[17] Nor could John Kmetz of Science Unlimited Research Foundation in San Antonio.[18]

Possible non-psi explanations for Backster's results include temperature fluctuations, humidity fluctuations, and excessively noisy equipment. Others speculate that Backster's results could be unconsciously caused by the experimenter himself. That is, he, rather than the plants, could be influencing the galvanometer readings through PK. Alternatively, it could be that his readings have found indication that plants do have an extremely primitive form of nervous system that is sensitive to life-threatening procedures.

Metal Bending

Three areas of alleged spontaneous psi have received considerable public interest. The first is metal bending by other than conventional means. Its most famous reported practitioner is the Israeli entertainer Uri Geller. Geller claims he is able to bend or break metal objects simply by holding them in his hands and stroking them. He has ostensibly demonstrated this ability on television. While Geller has submitted to some laboratory tests—such as the SRI test in which he drew the bunch of twenty-four grapes, indicating his ESP ability—there have been no successful controlled laboratory experiments reported in a professional journal to confirm his alleged metal-bending ability.

A few metal-bending cases did precede Geller. A family living in Bristol, England, in the latter half of the eighteenth century often found whole groups of pins tangled together into bizarre forms. A South Georgia family was reported in 1905 as finding their spoons bending or breaking when they sat down to meals.[19] And an Austrian medium active in the 1930s reportedly managed to cause mysterious scratches or dents to appear on metal objects placed on the table during her seances.[20]

One interesting report about Geller, by W. E. Cox, then of the Foundation for Research on the Nature of Man, appeared in the *Journal of Parapsychology.*[21] Cox, a former semi-professional magician, observed Geller in Geller's Manhattan apartment. Two keys were bent by Geller—allegedly through psychic powers—one to a 12½-degree angle and one to a 36-degree angle. One of the keys was bent while it was being held flat on a glass-topped table. Further, Cox brought with him a pocket watch he had jammed with a strip of tin foil. Geller shook the watch and it started running. When Cox opened the watch he found that the foil strip was broken in two and the speed regulator lever had moved several degrees. However, Geller has been unwilling to repeat this demonstration and has been criticized by other magicians and researchers who point out that metal bending and stage telepathy demonstrated by Geller can be duplicated by sleight-of-hand and conjuring tricks.

If metal-bending abilities do indeed exist, they may be caused by PK. Some experts believe that somehow the subject uses PK to manipulate the internal heat of an object, causing it to warp or bend. Others postulate that PK could manipulate the object's electromagnetic energy. Microwave radiation, the manipulation of cosmic radiation, and other forces have been considered as well.

Movement of Objects

A second area of claimed spontaneous psi currently of some public interest is the alleged movement of objects by other than ordinary means. In the heyday of mediums, the mysterious movement of objects was a common feature of seances. Often close study detected fraud on the medium's part, but, as R. H. Thouless observes, "There have, in fact, been a number of mediums who appeared to be able to produce movements of objects . . . in the presence of competent observers who were satisfied that the conditions were such that fraud was impossible."[22]

Perhaps the person most closely associated with this phenomenon at the present time is a Leningrad housewife named Nina Kulagina. No Western scientist has yet been permitted to research her professed abilities under controlled laboratory conditions. They would undoubtedly welcome the opportunity to do so because of reports received from scientists who have been permitted to observe her under *un*controlled conditions.

One such report discussed apparent movements of objects by Kulagina in J. G. Pratt's Leningrad hotel room.[23] Some of the objects she was apparently able to move, such as a matchbox, had been provided by Pratt and another observer. Others, such as a metal cylinder, were provided by the Russians. In his journal report of the incidents, Pratt evaluated the control conditions as good but not conclusive.

Some scientists suggest that, as in poltergeist disturbances involving movement, unconscious PK may be responsible for the apparent mysterious movement of these objects. Other observers hypothesize that the energy causing the movement is not a mental force but an unknown biological force, atmospheric energy force, or other force. Some Soviet scientists argue that the force moves the objects by nullifying gravity. They have coined the term *bioenergetics* to describe this process.

Psychophotography

A third area of alleged spontaneous psi of interest today is psychophotography. It is claimed that, by this process, images can be made to appear on photographic film or videotape without the use of any ordinary means. The first type of apparent psychophotography was called spirit photography. A photographer would photograph a client and find an extra face on the plate when it was developed. This extra face was often reported to resemble one of the client's deceased relatives.

The first known psychic (spirit) photograph was produced in 1862 by William Mumler of Boston. By the 1870s, spirit photography was being practiced in both the United States and England. Though many practitioners were exposed as frauds, some of them did produce pictures that were puzzling and could not be explained away easily.

Thoughtography, a name given to the direct impression of mental images on film or photographic plates, has been investigated both in Europe and in Asia. In Japan at the turn of the century, Professor T. Fukarai tested many subjects who could reportedly impress characters and pictures onto sealed photographic plates.[24]

One modern practitioner of psychophotography who has been extensively investigated in the laboratory is Ted Serios. Serios, a former Chicago bellhop who has had little formal education, has apparently been able to produce psychophotographic effects under controlled conditions in two laboratories.

One occurrence was at the University of Denver, and was reported by Jule Eisenbud in the *Journal of the American Society for Psychical Research*.[25+] In this test series Serios was apparently able to affect film by his mind alone. The object of the experiment was for Serios to attempt to make a picture of vehicles such as

The Russian sensitive Nina Kulagina with parapsychologist J. G. Pratt (Leningrad, October 1970).

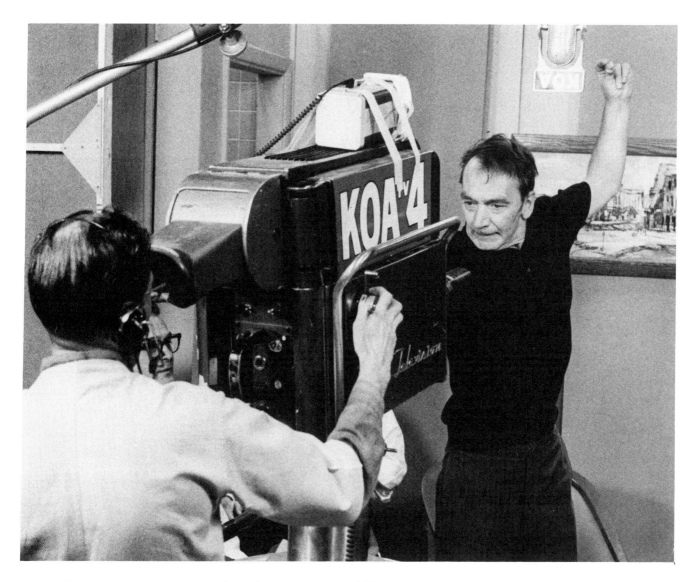

steam locomotives appear on Polaroid prints. Polaroid films, in two Polaroid cameras, were exposed one frame at a time at Serios' direction. Serios stared at the camera through a small black paper cylinder, about one inch in diameter. From time to time he signaled an experimenter to trigger the shutter. Of the 117 photographs taken with the camera, eight vehiclelike images (e.g., motorcycles) showed up on the film. Ten *blackies* also appeared; these are dark prints that appear when the film is developed and are considered evidence of something unusual. If nothing extraordinary had occurred, an image of the person looking into the lens would have appeared on the film.

Another report came from Ian Stevenson and J. Gaither Pratt, who conducted two separate studies with Serios at the University of Virginia and successfully replicated Eisenbud's findings.[26+] In one session Serios said he would attempt to project a part of Monticello, Thomas Jefferson's home, on the film. The fifty-six attempts produced several blackies and six possible images, all of columns or a cagelike structure. The researchers thought one of the images resembled a section of Monticello.

Ted Serios attempting to affect videotape through psychophotography.

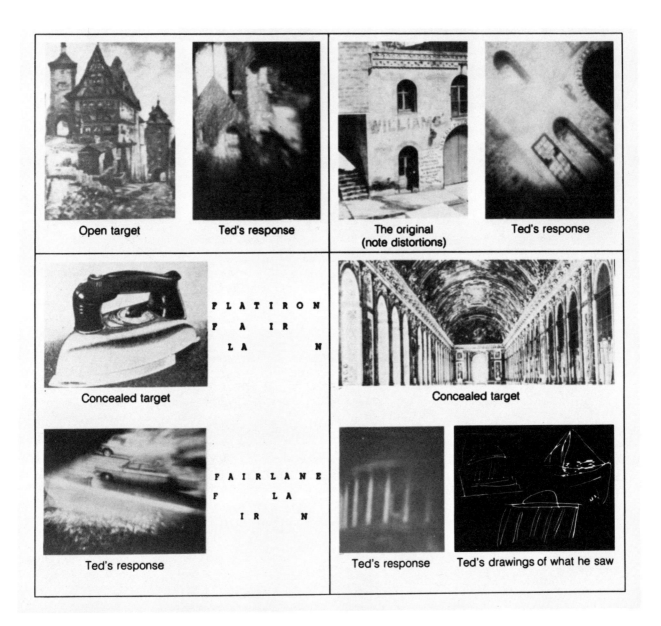

Samples of Ted Serios' work obtained by researcher Jule Eisenbud.

About his and Stevenson's work with Serios, Pratt has written:

If Ted is a fraud, a single clumsy action, one slip-up, would have been enough to expose him. Yet the fact is that no one among all the witnesses of Ted's successful shots has ever reported any direct observation giving evidence against the para-normal interpretation. This is an aspect of the case deserving serious consideration. In my judgment, it is enough to keep the question regarding Ted Serios specifically and psychic photography generally open for further scientific investigation.[27]

After completing the four experimental studies described above, Serios suddenly stopped producing any images at all. Today he is reported to have partially regained his ability and is being tested again in Eisenbud's studio, away from press and public exposure.

If psychophotography is real, it is likely that psychic photographers are using their own psychic ability to produce the results. Or perhaps they are using some sort of force that manipulates the particles on the film. It could be that they are creating some invisible form in front of the lens of the camera, which, in turn, is actually being photographed and printed on the film. Despite all the work that has been done on psychophotography, no general conclusions of any kind have yet been reached.

Survival and Consciousness

Two subjects traditionally associated with psychic phenomena have recently enjoyed a revival of public interest. They are survival and consciousness. The first of these, survival, concerns one of the most tantalizing of all human concepts—the possibility of life after death. Do human beings survive in some form after their bodies undergo physical death? Despite years of research, little is certain.

Much of the work done by early psychical researchers in connection with apparitions, hauntings, and mediums attempted to determine whether or not humans survived bodily death. Similarly, J. B. Rhine sought evidence bearing on the survival question in his early research. All these efforts ended in ambiguity.

In more recent times, the psychologist Karlis Osis has searched for clues to survival in descriptions of OBEs and deathbed reports. William Roll of the Psychical Research Foundation has also done extensive investigative work in this area. He calls the question of the continuation of consciousness beyond death the "most profound mystery of man's universe."[28] Ian Stevenson, as described in Chapter 12, looks at the subject in reincarnation studies.

Much attention has been given to the work of psychiatrist Elisabeth Kubler-Ross. Based on her extensive work with dying patients, Kubler-Ross has publically stated that she is convinced there is life after death.[29] Her claims are based in great part on reports from patients who have been resuscitated after coming close to death. Some of these patients have described leaving their physical bodies, traveling through a long, dark tunnel, and having remarkable encounters with the spirits of their deceased relatives. Similar reports have been described in the popular book, *Life After Life*,[30] by Raymond Moody, M.D., a former philosophy professor and now a psychiatrist.

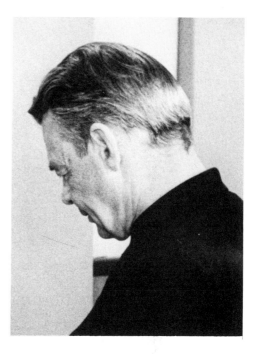

Jule Eisenbud of the University of Denver, one of the scientists who studied Ted Serios.

No scientific evidence of survival has been offered to support these subjective reports. Indeed, Moody has stated that his reports, in his opinion, do not represent conclusive evidence of life after death.[31] Perhaps they are due to people's conditioning as to the nature of death, leading them to have these experiences and then "come back" to report them. Near death, the brain's physiology can become strongly altered in ways that may lead to unusual hallucinatory experiences. Kubler-Ross's work has not been related to parapsychology, nor has she been involved in parapsychological investigations.

At the turn of the century, psychologist William James observed that our normal waking consciousness is surrounded by "potential forms of consciousness entirely different."[32] With the rise of the behaviorist approach to psychology, this viewpoint was largely ignored. But in recent times many people have become intrigued by the study both of consciousness and of altered states of consciousness. Some believe that the study of consciousness may yield answers to a number of perplexing mysteries, including those contained within psi.

Among those currently investigating consciousness are neuroscientist Karl Pribram of Stanford University and physicist David Bohm of the University of London, who propose that the human brain may be a hologram, interpreting a holographic universe.[33]

Robert Ornstein has called upon psychologists to return to consciousness study, saying that "psychology is primarily the science of consciousness."[34] A number of scientists disagree. Charles Tart, the University of California psychologist whose work in consciousness is well known, says that because words and definitions are only a small part of consciousness, "consciousness is inherently undefinable."[35]

While there is tremendous popular interest in the possibility of uncovering the meaning of consciousness, to date—as with survival—little is known with certainty. As Tart views it, perhaps a good way to study the ultimate nature of consciousness is through the study of psi. Indeed, he feels that the question, "Is consciousness nothing but brain functioning or is there something else?" may well be answered in the course of psi research.[36]

UFOs, Pyramids, and Spirit Recordings
A number of other topics have been sensationalized in the popular press and often associated with psi, but without scientific justification. Three of these are UFOs, pyramids, and spirit recordings.

Unidentified flying objects are just that, though they are held by some to represent intelligent beings from outer space or from other levels of reality. According to Jacques Vallee, computer expert and a leading authority on UFOs, "In the last twenty-five years, at least five thousand sightings of unidentified flying objects have been filed away, none explained by competent investigators . . . but no bridge has yet been built between this body of data and the evidence that exists for psychic phenomena such as PK, prophecy, and telepathy."[37]

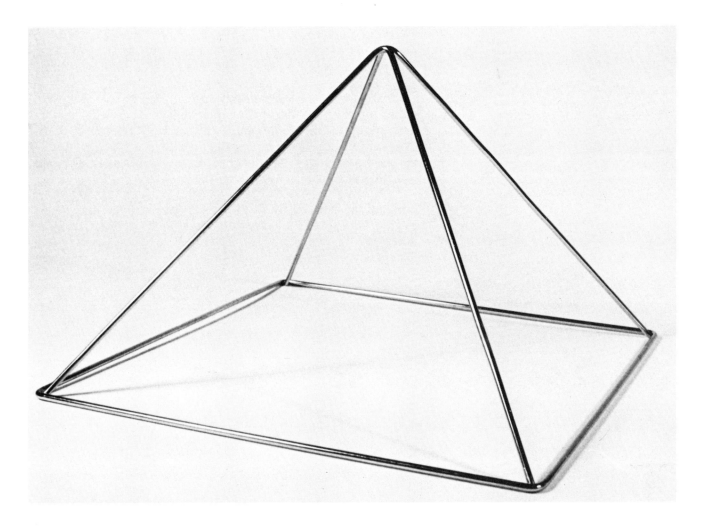

A pyramid.

While most flying objects can be ultimately identified as natural objects such as planes, birds, balloons, meteors, and bright stars, about 5–20 percent of the sightings are not identifiable as any known object or craft.[38] A recent poll of members of the American Astronomical Association found that 28 percent believed they had observed a UFO, and 80 percent considered UFOs worthy of scientific study.[39] The UFO controversy is probably more properly studied by exobiologists, astronomers, and psychologists than by parapsychologists.

There are people who believe that pyramid-shaped structures can influence the preservation and growth of organisms, alter the consciousness of a person who sits inside them, and even sharpen razor blades. But no scientific documentation of any of these claims can be found. A few researchers, including A. R. G. Owen,[40] have conducted experiments with pyramids and living material, but without observing any significant effects.

With the aid of a tape recorder, microphone, and radio, some claim to have recorded on tape the voices of the dead. These efforts are called spirit recordings. Though Konstantin Raudive, the Swedish psychologist, reported detecting some 25,000 voices from a mass of recorded material,[41] no positive findings on spirit recordings have been published in any scientific journals. Despite all the recent technological advances, despite all the individual reports, and despite all the public interest, still nothing is definitively known.

Most of these new interests rely on technological developments either for their creation or for their detection. Yet despite this technology, definitive laboratory evidence to demonstrate that even one of these areas represents a manifestation of psi has not yet been obtained. Biofeedback looks promising as an aid to psi use, but its promise has so far not been realized.

Some of the new or revived interests covered here may be psi-related, but a great deal of research remains to be done before the questions that currently exist about all of these areas can be resolved.

13.
Possible Applications of Psi

Businesses have been offered ESP scales as a tool to help them select employees; athletic coaches hold pregame meditation warmups; some of the seriously ill bypass conventional surgery in favor of psychic surgery. Right now, consumer uses of psi appear to be in the exploratory stage. Little is known, although much is promised. And yet strange things do appear to take place.

Probably the most promising area of the possible application of psi is in healing. Unexplained, spontaneous healings do occur. Sensitives have been shown in laboratory studies to have special healing abilities. J. B. Rhine has written that some forms of unorthodox healing may be psi-related: "The PK hypothesis may help to explain these strange organic occurrences."[1]

Public interest has far outstripped what is known or understood. This chapter will examine five general areas where psi may or may not be involved. They are creativity and business; information gathering; education; healing; and coincidences in daily life. Researchers continue to pose the same questions about each: is this related to what is called psi? If so, how? If not, then what is it?

The singer Della Reese.

Creativity and Business

Creativity may be related to psi. Some creative people report that they feel as if they have access to a realm of knowledge that is greater than normal. This is similar to the feeling reported by those who have had a psi experience. No definite relationship between the two has yet been demonstrated, although a number of studies have been done.

Two examples of the creative feeling come from the popular singer Della Reese and the inventor William Lear. Reese, who links her creativity with her strong belief in the power of God, says: "When I want to be especially creative, I don't try to do anything. I just open myself up and let go. . . . I think we all get communications we don't understand."[2]

Lear, whose many inventions include the Lear jet, says, "In designing an airplane, I use an awful lot of intelligence from other sources. . . . I have to visualize something and if I visualize it, then I can anticipate it so keenly that I actually feel I'm doing it."[3]

There are instances in which a creative piece of work appears to display precognitive qualities. For instance, Jonathan Swift's 1726 description of the moons of Mars in *Gulliver's Travels* can be closely compared to the actual moons that were discovered over a century after he wrote his imaginary description of them.

William Lear, inventor of the Lear jet.

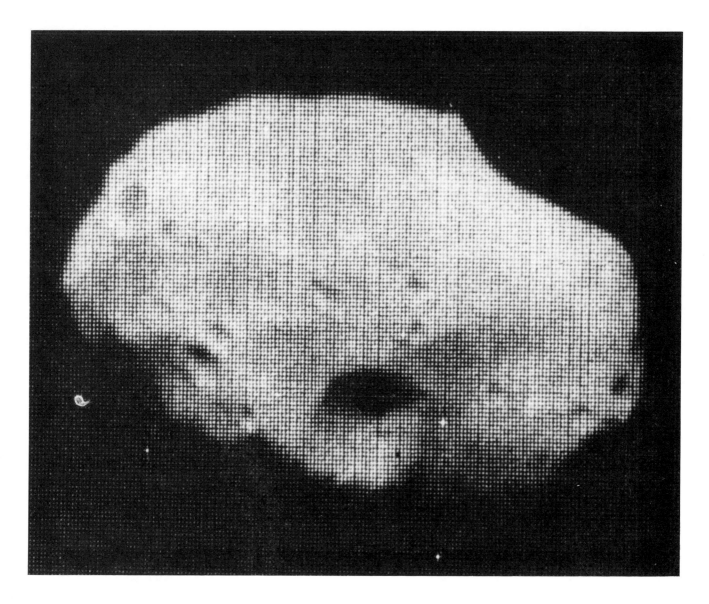

One of the satellites of Mars. Almost 200 years before they were discovered, their existence was predicted in 1726 in *Gulliver's Travels*.

Swift wrote: "They have likewise discovered two lesser stars, or satellites, which revolve about Mars, whereof the innermost is distant from the centre of the primary planet exactly three of his diameters, and the outermost five; the former revolves in the space of ten hours, and the latter in twenty-one and a half."[4]

Two tiny satellites were actually found 151 years later whose distances from Mars' center are 1½ diameters and 3½ diameters, and whose revolution periods are 7 hours 39 minutes and 30 hours 18 minutes, respectively. Martin Davidson, editor of *Astronomy for Every Man*, called Swift's description "the most extraordinary piece of guess-work in literature."[5] Bradford Smith, Associate Professor of Planetary Sciences at the University of Arizona at Tucson, says, "The similarity between these satellites and those mentioned in Swift's *Gulliver* is truly remarkable."[6]

A second example of seemingly precognitive creativity comes from a comparison (see accompanying table) of the novel *The Wreck of the Titan*, written in 1898 by Morgan Robertson, and the actual sinking of the oceanliner *Titanic* fourteen years later.[7]

Comparison of *Titan* and the *Titanic*

	The Novel *Titan*	The Ship *Titanic*
Month of sailing	April	April
Name of the ship	Titan	Titanic
Number on board	3,000	2,207
Number of lifeboats	24	20
Reason for sinking	Hit iceberg	Hit iceberg
Speed at impact with iceberg	25 knots	23 knots
Length	800 feet	882.5 feet
Displacement tonnage	75,000	66,000
Number of propellers	3	3
Reputation	Unsinkable	Unsinkable
Reason for high loss of life	Too few lifeboats	Too few lifeboats

An artist's conception of the sinking of the *Titanic*.

Thelma Moss of the University of California at Los Angeles, whose research indicates that artists may have psi abilities superior to those of nonartists.

Laboratory testing of the relationship between psi and creativity has yielded positive but not conclusive results. In research conducted at the University of California at Los Angeles, Thelma Moss showed that artists were able to score better on ESP tests than nonartists.[8+] Working with J. A. Gengerelli in another experiment, Moss discovered that psi transmission between a sender and a subject was extremely strong when at least one of the two was an artist of some sort.[9+] And Charles Honorton, in a test of randomly chosen high school students, found that students who had high scores on tests measuring creativity were significantly better able to make ESP predictions than were those students who scored poorly on the creativity test.[10]

Another possible relationship exists between successful business people and psi. Two businessmen who claim they have often been guided by strong intuitive hunches in making business decisions are William W. Keeler, recently retired board chairman of Phillips Petroleum, and Alexander M. Poniatoff, founder and Chairman of the Board emeritus of Ampex Corporation. Poniatoff says, "In the past I would not admit to anyone, especially business people, why my decisions sometimes were contrary to any logical judgment. But now that I have become aware of others who follow intuition, I don't mind talking about it."[11]

Keeler says of his career, "There were too many incidents that couldn't be explained merely as coincidences. I had successes in uncharted areas. My strong feelings towards things were accurate when I would let myself go." About ESP and the oil industry in general, Keeler says, "Oil fields have been found on hunches, through precognitive dreams, and by people who didn't know anything about geology."[12]

A test of businessmen by Douglas Dean and John Mihalasky of the Newark College of Engineering showed that executives of highly successful companies did better at tests of precognitive psi than did those whose companies were making only average earnings.[13] No definite conclusion can be made, however, concerning any relationship between business success and psi use. If psi does play a role in business success, it is almost definitely just one of a number of important factors, such as a person's financial, organizational, and managerial abilities.

Alexander M. Poniatoff, founder of the Ampex Corporation.

Detection

A second major area of what might be psi application is in information gathering or detection. When people want to find a source of water deep under the ground, or a ruin covered over by centuries of debris and dirt, or a murderer who has escaped from the scene of a crime, they sometimes turn to one of three techniques that may be psi-related. Although their psi-relatedness has not yet been demonstrated through scientific testing, these techniques are apparently sometimes quite effective.

Probably the best known detection technique is dowsing. Dowsers generally search for something—usually water underneath the earth's surface—with the aid of a hand-held device known as a dowsing rod or divining rod. This device can be a forked stick or it can be one of a number of other implements. Perhaps the earliest indication of dowsing comes from some eight thousand-year-old cave paintings discovered by French archaeologists in the Atlas Mountains. One of these shows a dowser, with what looks like a divining rod in hand, surrounded by a group of people.[14]

Many modern-day dowsers belong to the American Society of Dowsers, Inc., a nonprofit, educational and scientific society with membership open to all interested people. Their annual convention is held every September in Danville, Vermont, where nearly every year the dowsers' field trips allegedly produce new water

A dowser at work.

wells. According to the society, the practice of dowsing has been used to locate everything from booby traps to water mains. In Vietnam engineer units of the First and Third Marine Divisions reportedly used rods made from bent coat hangers to locate enemy tunnels, booby traps, and mines. Training sites were allegedly set up in Marine camps to teach troops dowsing before they went overseas.

While verification is almost impossible to obtain from groups or individuals employing dowsers, the society claims that its members are often hired by utility companies to identify the precise location of underground telephone cables, water mains, and electrical power lines. Some oil companies allegedly also employ dowsers. Other reported uses of dowsing include locating impurities in foodstuffs and organic and inorganic materials, and diagnosing unusual conditions of the body.[15]

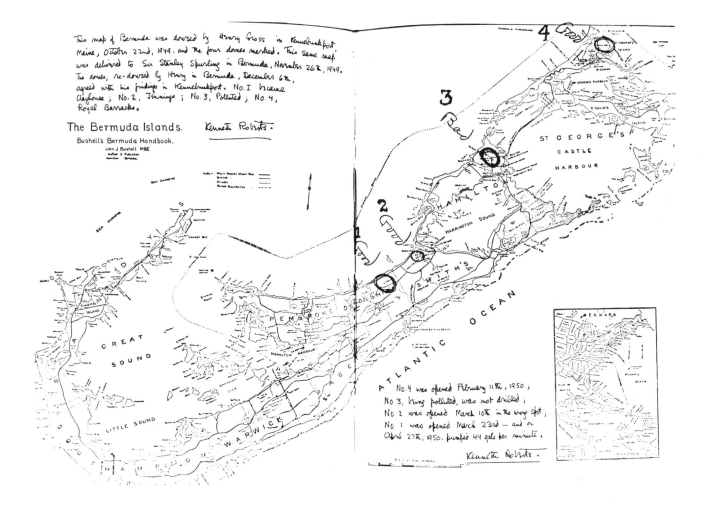

This map of Bermuda was dowsed by Henry Gross in Kennebunkport Maine, October 22nd, 1949, and the four domes marked. This same map was delivered to Sir Stanley Spurling in Bermuda, November 26th, 1949. The domes, re-dowsed by Henry in Bermuda, December 6th, agreed with his findings in Kennebunkport. No. I became Clayhouse ; No. 2, Jennings ; No. 3, Polluted ; No. 4, Royal Barracks.

The Bermuda Islands.   Kenneth Roberts.

Bushell's Bermuda Handbook.
John J. Bushell MBE
Author & Publisher
Hamilton Bermuda

No. 4 was opened February 11th, 1950 ;
No. 3, being polluted, was not drilled ;
No 2 was opened March 10th in the wrong spot ;
No 1 was opened March 23rd — and on
April 27th, 1950. pumped 44 gals per minute.

Kenneth Roberts.

**Map of Bermuda showing results of Gross'
map dowsing studies.**

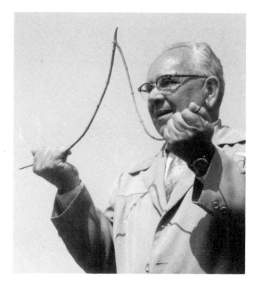

**Henry Gross, who reportedly found water
on the island of Bermuda while map dowsing at a dinner party in Maine.**

Another kind of dowsing, which may not be related in any way to the kind just described, is map dowsing. Probably the most dramatic case of reported map dowsing is that of dowser Henry Gross who, from his home in Kennebunkport, Maine, allegedly located three water wells on the island of Bermuda, eight hundred miles away. Novelist Kenneth Roberts, who wrote about the Gross case in *Henry Gross and His Dowsing Rod,* reports that the incident began at a party. A dinner conversation about Bermuda (which happened at that time to be drought stricken) prompted the gifted dowser to spread out a map of that island. Passing his divining rod over it, Gross promptly located four areas where he claimed fresh water could be found—despite the convictions of geologists that no fresh water existed on the island. Several months later, in April 1950, wells were located in three of the four locations Gross had predicted, furnishing Bermudans with ample fresh water not only for themselves but also for visiting ships needing supplies.[16]

In spite of the many reports of successful dowsing and the widespread nature of the practice, relatively little research has been carried out to evaluate it scientifically. It is difficult—indeed, almost impossible—to make a dependable evaluation of individual cases. Some individual dowsers' work has been well documented, but researchers are presently unable to determine how much information the successful dowsers might have received

A demonstration by Raymond C. Willey of
map dowsing done with a pendulum.

from their normal perception of the terrain. Chance cannot be
estimated in well digging, and controlled tests are hard to set up in
the field.

Some preliminary tests have been undertaken, however, and
dowsers have been able to determine, under controlled conditions, whether or not water was flowing in underground pipes,
and to locate hidden coins and other objects.[17+] Karlis Osis conducted a study of dowsing for concealed metal pipes using brass
rods, and of dowsing for concealed coins using hand-held pen-
dulums. These procedures produced statistically significant results. A long distance pendulum procedure, similar to map dowsing techniques, produced only chance results overall.[18] In other
tests dowsers have also failed to locate buried targets. Much
research still needs to be done on dowsing abilities.

Several possible explanations exist for dowsing. Most researchers agree that the movement of the forked stick or bent rod is
due to unconscious muscular action on the part of the dowser—
tiny muscle movements that the instrument amplifies. Thus some
kind of information is being obtained and expressed through the
dowsing rod. Dowsers may be making educated guesses by judg-

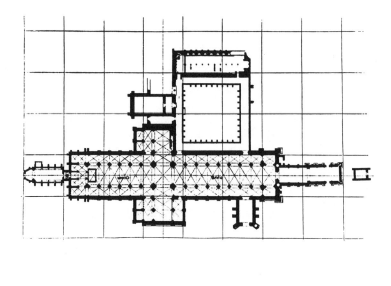

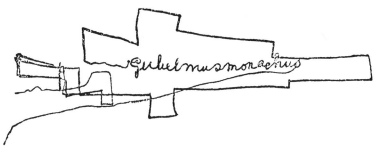

(Top) The excavated ruins of Glastonbury Abbey. (Bottom) J. Alleyne's automatic writings describing the site before it was excavated.

ing the terrain. Or they may be sensitive to fluctuations in the earth's magnetic field caused by the electromagnetic effects of flowing water or of underground minerals. One study, done by Dr. Zaboj Harvalik, a physicist and former advisor to the U. S. Army's Advanced Concepts Material Agency, indicates that many people may be able to detect weak magnetic fields by the skillful manipulation of dowsing rods.[19+]

Alternatively, a dowser may be detecting the presence of water or the target object by using psi, and be responding through muscular action, rather than through guesses, words, drawings, or hunches.

Another field where unusual detection techniques are sometimes used is archaeology. Some sensitives have reportedly identified sites that yielded fruitful archaeological findings, provided insight into the chronology of archaeological sites, and even described the origin of archaeological materials discovered at the site. In recent years the American Anthropological Association has held conferences on parapsychology and anthropology.

Frederick Bligh Bond, who worked on excavating England's Glastonbury Abbey in the early 1900s, wrote that he had been helped by automatic writings given him by a sensitive named John Alleyne.[20] More recently, Jeffrey Goodman described what he considered to be significant assistance given him in field work for his doctoral degree at the University of Arizona by a psychic named Aron.[21] According to Goodman, Aron helped him locate and describe a new primitive archaeological site at Flagstaff, Arizona. Aron selected the site and correctly predicted thirty-two of its thirty-four geological features and the depth at which tools and artifacts would be found.

An example of a psychic's reported ability to describe the origin of an artifact comes from Professor N. J. Emerson of the University of Toronto, a past president of the Canadian Archaeological Association.[22] Emerson took a black carved stone artifact discovered during the excavation of Iroquois Indian materials in Ontario to a psychic named George for examination. Emerson thought the artifact came from British Columbia because it was made of argillite, a stone available there. George, however, said that the artifact had been carved by a black person born and raised in Africa, who had been taken as a slave to the New World. Emerson, highly skeptical of George's theory, took the artifact to three other psychics. Each had no knowledge of George's theory; each separately came to the same conclusion. Upon checking with an African art expert, Emerson learned that the carving fit into the art styles of the Gold Coast region of Africa during the period the psychics claimed the carver had lived.

About the results, Emerson wrote:

> I am now convinced that it can be argued that intuitive or psychic knowledge does stand as a viable alternative to knowledge obtained by the more traditional methods of science. By utilizing a psychic team, and by cross analysis of their independent statements which reveal an amazing degree of correspondence and concurrence, I am convinced that we have been able to abstract intuitive truth about man's past . . . we have gone far beyond the limits of chance and coincidence as an explanation.[23]

J. N. Emerson (left) and Jeffrey Goodman (right). Both archaeologists report they have been helped in their work by psychics.

Another field where unusual detection techniques are sometimes used is in police work. Gerard Croiset, a Dutchman, is probably one of the best known and most successful investigators of this type. Studied for his apparent clairvoyant abilities by parapsychologists at Utrecht University, Croiset has worked with European police for twenty-five years.

One example of the way Croiset works can be found in a 1960 case involving a missing child. Upon hearing a description of the child and where he was last seen, Croiset reportedly said, "I see three dikes—they must be roads—coming together. . . . I see a tunnel . . . and near it, a small storehouse with a steel door. I also see a culvert. . . . I see a slope of stone, a lot of concrete and new cement on a bridge. Near that small tunnel you will find the child lying in the water . . . his fishing rod near him."[24] The police identified a location that appeared to match Croiset's description and found the boy's body there the next day. All of the landmarks Croiset described were correct: the three roads, the storehouse, the concrete bridge, the tunnel, and the culvert. William Gorter, chief of police in Haarlem, has been quoted as saying, "I've worked with Croiset for some years and in several cases he's had amazing successes. His ability is unquestioned."[25]

Another comment on the use of psi in crime detection was made by the late Pat Price, former police commissioner of Burbank, California, and (as was seen in Chapter 8) a highly successful

Gerard Croiset, a psychic who has allegedly helped various police forces on a number of occasions.

subject in remote-viewing psi at Stanford Research Institute. Price said, "As police commissioner I used my abilities to track down suspects, although at the time I couldn't confront the fact that I had these abilities, and laid my good fortune to intuition and luck."[26]

Psychics are by no means totally correct or even partially correct all the time. Often their reports are completely incorrect. Alternative explanations for successful psychic detection range from mind reading to fraud. Few official documents attesting to a joint effort of police and psychics are available.

A final unusual form of detection involves the Central Premonitions Registry. The registry, headed by Robert D. Nelson, is located in New York City.[27] The concept underlying the registry is to identify individuals who are proven consistently correct in forecasting events and to eventually serve as a kind of early-warning system to detect disasters before they occur.

One of the most striking cases recorded at the Central Premonitions Registry is that of a woman who accurately predicted the attempted assassination of Alabama Governor George Wallace, even to the details of the suit he was wearing and where the blood showed on his clothes. According to the registry, this experience so frightened the woman reporting it that she has refrained from sending in any other predictions and has forbidden the registry to identify her publicly.

The registry, in operation since 1968, makes no claims that the reported premonitions it receives are valid, correct, or psi-related. It serves simply as a recording agency where reports are on file for possible later analysis. The original registry idea came from Great Britain, which still has its own registry. The Toronto Society of Psychical Resarch has been serving a similar function for Canada since 1971. No formal evaluation has yet been made of the total material, and no conclusions have been drawn on the basis of these registries as to the occurrence or reliability of reported instances of spontaneous premonition.

Education

Although much public interest has been attracted to the possible application of psi to education, to date only a tiny amount of work has been done in this area. Few parapsychologists have made any attempt to test the involvement of psi in an educational setting. Many conservative educators are reluctant to investigate the possibility of psi in the classroom.

A study reported in 1958 by Margaret Anderson and Rhea White, then of Duke University, examined the relationship between students' attitudes toward their teacher and their success at psi testing.[28] The results showed that there does appear to be a clear correlation between the two. High ESP scores occurred when both teacher and pupil liked each other, low ESP scores occurred when both disliked each other, and chance scores were found when only one member of the pair liked the other. While the experiments were not designed to determine if there was any relationship between academic performance and psi ability, an analysis of results showed that students who received higher class grades also obtained higher ESP scores.

Two experiments conducted in recent years explored the relationship between students' personality traits and ESP test success. Psychiatrist Gerald Jampolsky at the Child Study Center in Tiburon, California, obtained test results that tentatively indicate that hyperactive children may sometimes have more paranormal traits than normal children.[29+]

Results of a series of exploratory tests conducted by Eloise shields indicate that there may be a relationship between certain personality traits and success at ESP tests.[30+] She found that children who were determined by psychological tests to be personally "withdrawn" did relatively poorly on ESP tests, while "not withdrawn" children did relatively well on ESP tests. Other divisions by sex, intelligence, and age gave no significant differences. Shields, a school psychologist in a public school district in Los Angeles County and a parapsychologist, said in her report of the test results, "Indications are that children who are not withdrawn can, in general, guess better or more successfully demonstrate their ESP ability by hitting the target than chance alone can reasonably explain. Psychologically withdrawn children, on the other hand, appear to show a tendency to guess consistently below the chance level, or to exhibit psi-missing."[31]

One experiment reported in 1972 by psi researcher Martin Johnson, then of Lund University in Sweden, should be of interest to students facing school examinations. Johnson embedded an ESP test in the final exam for a course he was teaching in psychology. He hoped to approximate a real-life setting by keeping the students unaware that they were taking an ESP test. For some of the exam questions, Johnson wrote out and concealed correct answers to serve as psi targets. For other questions, Johnson did not prepare any correct answers. The students appeared to be able to use ESP to boost their test scores: they scored better on questions for which Johnson had written out correct answers than they did on questions for which he had not.[32]

The results of these experiments and others like them remain fragmentary at the present time. No clear connection between psi abilities and educational success or failure has yet been demonstrated. However, it seems likely that psi may be present in the classroom to some degree.

Healing

Anyone who has experienced serious illness, or even a violently upset stomach, knows of the overwhelming desire for good health that seizes a sick person. The search for a cure takes on an intensity and passion virtually unsurpassed in human existence.

The possible correlation of psi to healing is probably the most intriguing and promising of all the phenomena associated with psi. Potentially of direct benefit to all of humanity, the instances of healing caused by unknown means precipitate psi investigations and often stimulate funding of psi research. While some instances of unusual healing do occur, no one knows whether or not psi is involved.

Modern-day practitioners of orthodox medicine are highly aware of the close relationship between patients' mental and emotional states and their physical condition. "Perhaps 90 percent of the patients I see in my office," says Dr. Franklin K. Paddock, a distinguished specialist in internal medicine who practices in Pittsfield, Massachusetts, "suffer directly or indirectly from psychosomatic illness."[33] A number of laboratory studies have shown that patients sometimes report their physical condition has been dramatically, although temporarily, improved when, unbeknownst to them, the healing "medicine" they were given was nothing more than a placebo, a sugar pill. Such illnesses as ulcers, asthma, and certain skin disorders are viewed by many physicians as at least partly emotional in origin in many cases. There is even some preliminary work currently underway to explore whether or not there may be a relationship between emotional states and certain forms of cancer.[34]

But are there forms of healing that go beyond the effects of psychosomatic treatment? Stories and reports of faith healing and psychic healing seem to suggest that diseases can be diagnosed and healing can take place without the usual medical assistance that most people accept as necessary today. This is not a new idea. Many early societies and primitive religions had medical treatments that may have psi components.

Long before people developed the science of healing known as medicine, they practiced certain magic and religious arts to restore health. As early as 3000 B.C., such practices were recorded in

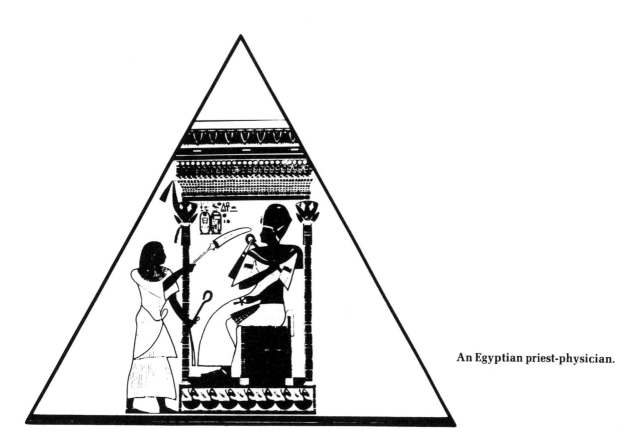

An Egyptian priest-physician.

widely separated areas from Siberia to isolated areas of South America. In Egypt the tomb of the deified Imhotep, chief physician to King Zoser about 2980 B.C., was for many centuries a place of pilgrimage for sick people seeking a cure. Other shrines with alleged healing properties honored such priest-physicians as Thrita in Persia, Dhan-Wantari in India, and Aesculapius in Greece. Many successful cures at the Shrine of Aesculapius were effected by means of dreams. After sufferers visited the shrine and prayed for healing, a god would appear to the patients in their dreams and treat the disease.[35]

The healings recorded in the Bible are well known, and the custom of *laying-on-of-hands* dates from at least biblical times. Healing of the sick played a central role in the early history of Christianity, but after about A.D. 250 only traces of this work can be found.

The importance people place on health was reflected in the special healing powers ascribed by many nations to their kings, whom they believed divinely descended or anointed. A disease known as The King's Evil was believed in the Middle Ages to be curable only by the touch of a reigning sovereign. King Louis IX of France was considered so powerful a healer that he was hailed as St. Louis.

Certainly today many cultures practice unconventional methods of healing. In parts of Africa witch doctors are expected to give a correct diagnosis of illness without being told anything about the symptoms and even without seeing the patient. In the Philippines many alleged practitioners of psychic healing focus on the concept of purification. They believe that if patients can be

A Cuna Indian healer, shown with his medicine book and medicine dolls.

An American Indian medicine man.

cleansed of physical and spiritual impurities during the healing ritual, they will be restored to health.[37] In Great Britain the National Federation of Spiritual Healers has been granted the right to help treat patients in that country's fifteen hundred national hospitals if the patient requests their services and the attending physician gives permission.[38] In Panama's San Blas Islands, if a Cuna Indian is too ill to travel to the healer, the diagnosis is made from a doll sent to the healer by the patient.[39] In Brazil psychic

An artist's conception of a mesmerist at work with a patient.

An Eighteenth-Century Cure-All

Hailed as a means of curing all manner of physical ailments, Mesmerism was founded by Anton Mesmer, an eighteenth-century Viennese physician. He specialized in treating patients with metal wands by which magnetic fluids in the body supposedly responsible for illness could allegedly be manipulated. By waving these wands over sufferers' bodies, Mesmer achieved such extraordinary results that people came from all over Europe to be treated by him.

Observers today believe Mesmer's real achievement was to induce a mild form of hypnosis in those he treated.[36] Many mesmerized patients displayed unusual behavior patterns not unlike those found at old-fashioned revival meetings: they jumped up and down, they contorted their bodies, they fell unconscious to the ground, they made rapturous noises. And often they felt a great deal better after the experience. Recent research confirms that some people find their sufferings lessened if they are simply touched by a person in whose curative powers they believe. Mesmerism spread from its founder to a large number of other practitioners, and vestiges of these ideas can occasionally be seen at the present time.

healers of the Spiritist tradition believe their patients have two bodies, a physical one and a spiritual one. Orthodox medicine is often used to cure ailments in the physical body, but in conjunction with psychic healing and counseling to alleviate illness in the spiritual body.

Three studies of unconventional healing practices were recently funded by the National Institute of Mental Health (NIMH), one of the few instances in which the U. S. government has funded research in an area that may be associated with psi abilities. In the first study John Dick and Robert Bergman helped Navajo Indians train medicine people in traditional as well as orthodox medical practice. Navajo healing methods include trance, divination, ritual dance and songs, herbal medicine, family therapy, and spirit contact through sandpainting.[40] In a second study, Horace Stewart and his assistants examined forty Afro-American healers who used such techniques as laying-on-of-hands, prayer, and suggestion.[41+] Richard Katz, in a third study, investigated Kalahari bushmen of the ¡Kung tribe in Africa. The ¡Kung feel that most of their young men have healing potential. They use special dances and rituals to gain access to healing life energies.[42+]

Bernadette Soubirous, who allegedly saw a vision of the Virgin Mary in a cave in Lourdes, France.

Edgar Cayce, who reportedly possessed mysterious diagnostic and healing powers.

One of the better known approaches to nontraditional healing is found in Lourdes, France. The fame of Lourdes stems from the reported cures effected there after Bernadette Soubirous, an uneducated fourteen-year-old miller's daughter, in 1858 reportedly saw visions of the Virgin Mary in a cave. During one of Bernadette's visions, a spring purportedly gushed forth from the grotto, and it is the water from this spring that is credited as the vehicle for many cures at Lourdes. In 1933 Bernadette was made a saint by the Roman Catholic Church.

Since the report of her first vision, thousands of people have claimed that they were miraculously cured of such conditions as cancer, paralysis, and tuberculosis by bathing in the spring waters of the grotto, now a Catholic shrine. Patients are asked to bring medical certificates of their illnesses to Lourdes and, if one claims to be cured, the case is immediately examined by the Lourdes Medical Bureau. After a year has passed, a reported cure is further examined by the Lourdes International Medical Commission, a group composed of about forty physicians. If a case passes both of these tests, an advisory committee of doctors and churchmen decides whether the case is indeed "miraculous," that is, medically inexplicable. Only a tiny fraction of the claimed cures have been placed in this category. To be defined as miraculous, the cure must be sudden, instantaneous, and complete, and there must be no recurrence of the illness. Furthermore, the original illness must have been such that the cure obtained could not have been effected by ordinary medical means.[43]

Some Americans' first exposure to unorthodox methods of healing came from reading about Edgar Cayce (1877–1945), who reportedly possessed powers to help the sick. Cayce could allegedly put himself into an altered state of consciousness and then diagnose illnesses and outline treatments for strangers who were often hundreds of miles away.

Cayce, a professional photographer, had no medical training whatsoever, just a strong desire to help the sick. Over a forty-three-year period, Cayce endeavored to help more than eight thousand different people. In each instance he would enter a self-induced trance, be given a sick person's name and address, and dictate to a waiting stenographer his diagnosis and proposed course of treatment. Transcripts of these dictations were then sent to the person or to the attending physician for use in attempting to heal the patient.

The reports of Cayce's alleged abilities might be explained by the use of psi, facilitated by his self-induced trance state. His medical recommendations varied widely, from psychological suggestions, to herbs and foods, to specific chiropractic manipulations. Often the treatments were quite different from standard medical practice. However, in many of the case reports there was no follow-up to determine if his description and diagnosis were accurate for the individual in question. Nor did Cayce ever participate in formal tests for psi under controlled conditions, so there is no evaluation of his abilities under laboratory test conditions.

In the United States at the present time, there is increasing interest in psychic or paranormal healing. Many individuals—including sincere religious leaders, television personalities, psychics, people claiming occult powers, and outright charlatans—are currently engaging in allegedly psychic healing, with the more unscrupulous charging large sums of money for their services.

That many healings take place regardless of the character or abilities of the healer is not surprising, because many diseases respond to positive suggestion, improved states of mind, and belief in the power of the treatment. Indeed, one of the new trends in medicine today that uses such factors is called *holistic health*. Doctors, nurses, and others who practice holistic medicine attempt to work with individuals in all ways that relate to their health, including nutrition, exercise, social and religious beliefs, psychological and emotional reactions to disease, and self-responsibility. In addition to regular medical techniques, holistic health practitioners may use acupuncture, biofeedback training, meditation and relaxation, counseling, changes in diet, herbal remedies, and so-called psychic healing techniques. It is difficult to determine whether such unconventional healing techniques actually draw on psi abilities.

Edgar Cayce

Cayce allegedly first discovered his unusual healing powers at the age of twenty-one, when he developed a gradual paralysis of the throat muscles. Despite medical treatment, no cure was found, and it was feared he would lose his voice. As a last resort, a friend helped him enter a self-induced trance. In the trance state Cayce was reportedly able to outline a course of treatment for himself, which eventually relieved his symptoms.

Cayce's son, Hugh Lynn Cayce, describes what happened when a number of local physicians turned to Cayce for help in diagnosing their own patients. "They soon discovered that Cayce only needed to be given the name and address of the patient, wherever he was, and was then able to 'tune in' telepathically oh that individual's mind and body as easily as if they were both in the same room. . . . One of the young physicians, Dr. Wesley Ketchum, submitted a report on this unorthodox procedure to a clinical research society in Boston. On October 9, 1910, the *New York Times* carried two pages of headlines and pictures. From that day on, invalids from all over the country sought help from the 'wonder man.' "[44]

Cayce left well over fourteen thousand stenographic records of his "readings." These have been microfilmed and are on file with the Library of Congress. They are also made available to those interested through the Association for Research and Enlightenment, an extension of the Edgar Cayce Foundation in Virginia Beach, Virginia. An international study program continues to examine the Cayce readings.[45]

Beyond certainly genuine but not extraordinary effects, there are still some healings that may in fact involve psi. Lawrence LeShan, a clinical psychologist, suggests that the methods used in healing may be of two types. In type one the healer attempts to become receptive and merge with the patient into the universal harmony of the universe. Examples of this type are religious prayer and meditation. In type two the healer attempts to focus "energy" on the patient, or to concentrate on healing the individual. This type is illustrated by the technique of laying-on-of-hands.[46]

But an accurate assessment of psi involvement remains elusive, because the extent of the body's ability to repair itself spontaneously is not yet known. Techniques such as biofeedback training are demonstrating that human beings may regulate their bodies to a much greater extent than was previously believed. So a healing that appears extraordinary may be a normal human capacity, whether spontaneous, mobilized by suggestion, or catalyzed by psi. In any event, there are numerous reported cases in which healing occurs in a way contrary to medical expectations.

Because reports of healings are difficult to evaluate, like spontaneous cases of psi, some researchers are attempting to find means of studying them in the laboratory. Recent research results give strong indication that positive suggestions are not the only explanation for at least some instances of unconventional healing. Tests done with animals and biochemical systems not susceptible to verbal influences raise the possibility that psi may affect living tissues directly. One of the pioneers in this endeavor, whose work is recognized as a landmark in the field, is Dr. Bernard Grad of McGill University in Montreal. Two of his experiments studied the effect of the laying-on-of-hands by a healer, and their results appear to indicate that healers can effect organic changes by touch alone. In one experiment, animals in containers held by a healer recovered more rapidly from skin wounds than those in containers held by someone else, or those in containers that were gently heated.[47] In a second experiment, Grad investigated the effect of water treated by a healer upon the growth rate of plants. Barley seeds that received water from a bottle held between the hands of a healer grew faster than those that received nontreated water.[48]

Sister Mary Justa Smith at Rosary Hill College examined the ability of the same healer used in Grad's studies to influence the biological activity of the enzyme trypsin. Trypsin solution in bottles that he held between his hands became more active than before, whereas control solutions not held by him did not change their activity.[49] However, the results were not considered conclusive.

While associated with New York University, Dolores Krieger conducted a field study of a healer who worked with human patients rather than laboratory animals. She found that hemoglobin, an important component of blood, changed dramatically in treated individuals. The technique the healer used was laying-on-of-hands.[50] The experiment did not conclusively establish whether the changes were due to the treatment itself or to the individuals' altered outlook and lifestyle. A second experiment

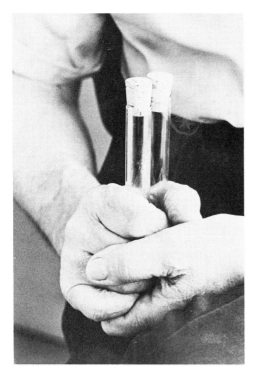

The healer holding a bottle of water in the Bernard Grad experiment.

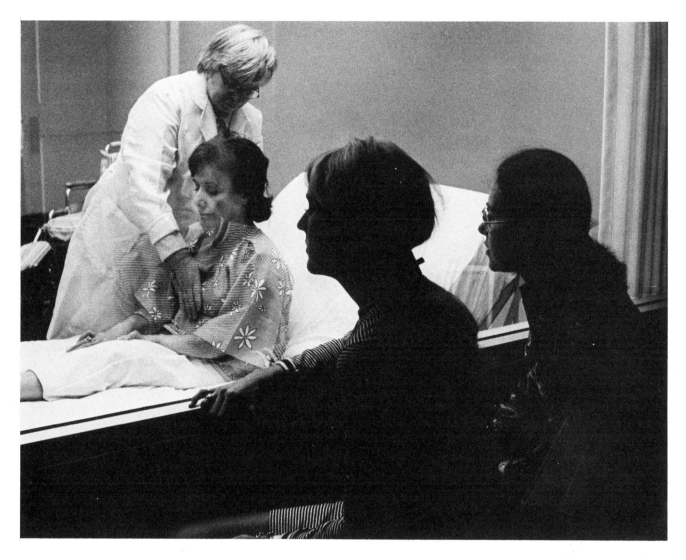

confirmed the hemoglobin change.[51] Again, however, variables such as altered outlook and lifestyle were not considered.

Following these studies, Krieger began working with a number of nurses across the United States, teaching them this technique. She has recently formed a membership organization of nurses to examine new ways of providing health-care services, including laying-on-of-hands.[52]

Another experiment in healing was done by Graham Watkins and Anita Watkins at the Foundation for Research on the Nature of Man in Durham, North Carolina, to study the effect of a sender's mental activity on the physical condition of animals. Subjects attempted to awaken a group of anesthetized mice by concentrating on them from the next room. All mice were equally anesthetized and divided into target and control groups. Mice that were concentrated upon awakened sooner than the control group of those that were not concentrated upon.[53] Two additional experiments by other researchers later confirmed this effect.[54]

Successful healings achieved by unorthodox means are subject to a number of alternative explanations. Because of the human body's amazing ability to heal itself, it is often difficult to separate

Dolores Krieger attempting to help a patient by the laying-on-of-hands.

Anita and Graham Watkins, who designed an experiment to test the effects of a sender on anesthetized mice.

normal from paranormal healing. Yet while the body's normal healing capacities and psychosomatic effects must be taken into account, the laboratory experiments imply that psi may also play a part in healing processes. If so, it would probably do so in the form of PK, since psychokinesis is the form in which psi affects matter. It may be that PK actually can change diseased or damaged tissue by manipulating or altering it. Or it may catalyze the body's normal restorative ability, precipitating or speeding up the process of healing. However, a great deal more research will have to be done on the topic of psychic healing before these questions are resolved.

Psi in Daily Life

Reports of psi in ordinary daily life indicate that psi may be more common than many people realize. C. D. Broad, a philosopher at Cambridge University, said, "If paranormal cognition or paranormal causation are facts . . . they may well be continuously operating in the background of our normal lives."[55]

J. R. Smythies, a physician at the Royal Edinburgh Hospital in Scotland, comments, "It's a plausible guess that many of our everyday thoughts and emotions are telepathic or partly telepathic in origin but are not recognized to be so because they are so much distorted and mixed with other mental contents in crossing the threshold of consciousness."[56]

Some researchers have tried to learn how frequently various types of spontaneous psi occur through surveys of the general public. Psychologist John Palmer surveyed the residents of Charlottesville, Virginia, and reported that more than a third of those who responded claimed to have had ESP experiences.[57]

Analysis of spontaneous reports has been going on since the earliest days of psychical research. Early British researchers sampled seventeen thousand people, asking if they had had an experience of seeing an apparition or hearing a voice without any physical cause—which might be a form of psi. Almost 10 percent said yes.[58]

Several parapsychologists have collected cases of alleged spontaneous psi experiences, and a study of these cases shows that the most common type of psi that occurs in them is precognition. Louisa Rhine analyzed 3,290 cases recorded and sent to the Duke University laboratory and found that 40 percent of them were precognitive.[59] She also found that the psi information—whether precognitive, telepathic, or clairvoyant—appeared most frequently to people in dreams. Less frequent forms were in waking intuitions or hallucinations.[60] While it is difficult to draw detailed conclusions from these studies, it seems possible that spontaneous psi may be quite common among the general population.

Rex Stanford has developed an experimentally testable model to evaluate reported spontaneous psi events.[61] Stanford's model attempts to speak to the seeming coincidences that dot most people's lives, as, for example, a person who thinks of a distant friend for the first time in some months and then receives a phone call out of the blue from the friend that same day; or a person who always seems to be able to find a parking space, no matter how crowded the streets. Many people have had letters cross in the mail or have unexpectedly run across someone they particularly wanted to see.

Stanford's theory is that people may be using psi all the time to scan the world around them, tuning in to individuals and events that are important for their needs. Although this is apparently done unconsciously, the information gained is used in conscious thoughts and behavior. Thus a person might arrive at a subway station just in time to encounter a business associate that he had been trying to telephone, or two people might pick up the telephone at the same time to call each other. Stanford suggests that psi could be responsible for these "coincidences."

About his theoretical model, not yet scientifically tested, Stanford has written, "among other things, it suggests that at least some of the seemingly meaningful events in life which we usually dismiss as 'sheer coincidence' may be psi-mediated and actively produced by the organism."[62+]

Stanford's theory suggests a new frontier in psi research. It implies that psi may be more common than has been previously thought; it is not only gifted subjects, the psychic superstars, who have psi, but they are simply persons who have learned to consciously develop and control their innate psi abilities. According

Psychologist Rex G. Stanford, who has developed a theory of psi in daily life.

to Stanford's theory it is possible that everyone has psi to some degree and that everyone uses it in daily life, even without realizing it. The validity of this theory remains to be tested.

The search for psi has just begun. No one can yet be sure where in human life psi is manifested, although a number of promising possibilities have already been identified. When researchers succeed in piecing together a picture of how psi works, then many of the mysteries described in this section should be resolved.

IV.
Reflections on the Search

Psi stands at a crossroads, its possible value for humanity just beginning to be explored. The few scientifically established facts that have been discovered about the subject are weighed down by the dual encumbrances of a dubious past and a sensationalized present. Until people are able to separate the realities of psi from the myths that surround it, an accurate assessment of its potential value will be impossible.

The study of psi requires professionalism of the highest order. It needs a place and a climate of its own in which to develop—away from the realm of the mystical and the atmosphere of the nightclub. It also needs patience, for the facts come slowly.

While some important research has been initiated, the effort to understand psi must receive widespread support if it is to have any real chance of success.

14.
Breaking
the Circle

Confusion about psi is pervasive and profound. The extent and depth of that confusion shocked us into spending over two years of our lives on this book, and into working with psi researchers in order to put this consensus statement together.

In the SEARCH section we looked at all the different ways psi may—or may not—be part of our lives. At this point we have no way of knowing what the applications of psi might be, despite all the tantalizing possibilities being explored. But if psi works, perhaps we can develop ways to make it of significant use in all of our lives. We think the potential benefits make a serious and concerted effort worthwhile.

We think the best things currently available to help us understand psi are the findings from the systematic laboratory investigations. Yet the laboratory study has a long way to go. If it is to be pursued vigorously—and we think it should be—it will need widespread, committed public support. Unfortunately, we think the present attitude toward psi has changed little since 1874, when Sir William Crookes said that psychic phenomena are viewed with "too easy credulity on the part of some people and equally irrational incredulity on the part of others."[1] We think it is time for all of us to move beyond questions of belief or disbelief, and we think supporting further scientific investigation may help us to do so.

There are a number of practical steps we feel should be taken if the possible benefits of psi are to be realized.

First, the phenomenon must be accepted as a legitimate field of study and that study must become a first-class citizen in the academic and scientific communities. There are some promising signs along this line. The Parapsychological Association and individual researchers are beginning to present symposia on psi before groups of the American Association for the Advancement of Science, the American Psychological Association, the American Psychiatric Association, the American Anthropological Association, and the Institute of Electrical and Electronics Engineers.[2]

The educational establishment is also beginning to open up, at least a bit, to psi. When we asked Joseph Platt, then President of Harvey Mudd College in California, how he felt about psi study, he said that if members of his faculty chose to do research in parapsychology he would not fault them for doing so. Glenn Olds, former President of Kent State University in Ohio, told us that he actively encourages his faculty to explore psi scientifically. As Dr.

Frederick Nicholson, Director of the American Museum of Natural History in New York City, emphasized to us, science is essentially a way of asking new questions. And many scientists and other observers agree that the new questions posed by psi study must be asked.

Further, there is growing openness among physicians and others involved with preventive health care toward nontraditional forms of healing. A recent three-day presentation on unorthodox healing by the Los Angeles Center for Integral Medicine was attended at the University of California by over 2,500 persons from all over the United States and Canada. Many orthodox professionals express openness to the concept of unconventional healing. As Alton Ochsner, M.D., founder of the Ochsner Clinic in New Orleans, says: "In all my years of practice I can conservatively say that fully 85 percent of the healings I was party to were unexplained."[3]

Yet much as we are encouraged by these promising trends, we see their frailty and vulnerability as well. And we see some major concerns.

Funding to support psi research is so small as to be almost nonexistent. A handful of large donations have come from wealthy individuals who left their fortunes to support the study of life after death. However, this area is not in the mainstream of present-day research. The U. S. government rarely sponsors psi research. The bulk of what little basic research support there is comes from a few small foundations and from private individuals.

Because there is almost no funding available, there is comparatively little research currently underway. Major investigation is actively in progress at only a few generally recognized psi laboratories around the world. These include the University of Freiburg in West Germany, Maimonides Medical Center in Brooklyn, the Foundation for Research on the Nature of Man in Durham, and the Stanford Research Institute.* Most of this research is fragmentary and lacking in continuity. Without prolonged systematic study, it is unlikely that a comprehensive theory about psi can be developed.

In the United States at the present time, with the exception of the University of Virginia, no college or university provides financial support for research into psi. Researchers employed at an institution of higher education must find psi research funding for themselves. One example of this situation is Robert Morris, lecturer in parapsychology at the University of California at Santa Barbara. His salary is paid not by that university but by a private foundation.

To compound this rather sad state of affairs, what few research findings are in hand have been poorly communicated to the scientific community and to the world at large. Consequently, the job of sifting out the results of serious legitimate research from the wealth of misinformation surrounding psi is extraordinarily difficult.

One reason the facts about psi are so hard to locate is related to the very name associated with the investigation of psi: para-

*A list of psi laboratories may be found in Appendix A.

psychology. It is ironic that a branch of science dedicated to the investigation of an unknown means of communication should be given a particularly uncommunicative name. Some people even think that the term refers to a psychologist's assistant in the same way that the term paralegal often refers to a lawyer's assistant.

And as for the title used by psi researchers—parapsychologist—its use is not restricted in any way. While such professional designations as lawyer, clinical psychologist, and doctor of medicine are carefully restricted to those who have successfully completed a demanding course of study and passed state licensing examinations, the title parapsychologist is available to anyone who wants to use it. Most scientists from other disciplines are careful to avoid the title parapsychologist and the term parapsychology. As a result, physicists are often unaware of parapsychological findings by physicians, biologists do not know of related work done by chemists, and the field is further fragmented.

Problems exist with the professional literature of parapsychology as well. Many scientists have been heard to ask, if parapsychology studies are valid, why don't we see them published in the established general science or educational periodicals? Unfortunately, with a few exceptions these influential periodicals have refused to publish research reporting positive evidence of psi. This refusal probably stems from the controversial nature of the field, the fraud long associated with psychic phenomena, and the editors' own lack of background in parapsychology. Nonetheless, the omission of reports on parapsychological investigations from these journals reinforces the skeptic's belief that psi does not exist and so cannot be studied. It also closes off a major avenue that researchers, scholars, and others use in order to obtain reliable information about a subject.

The situation facing the general public may be the worst of all. Because so few reliable sources for psi information exist, and because the study of psi in the laboratory is so highly technical, much of the information disseminated by news media is inaccurate and unreliable. Lack of expert advice also imperils the business of allocating grants for research. Virtually every panel asked to pass on research proposals has no parapsychological advisor to assist it. It is therefore particularly difficult for proposals for psi research to obtain funding. The Parapsychological Association is now twenty years old, but whatever professional counsel it can give is seriously curtailed by the fact that it is short-staffed and underfunded. Indeed, few people are even aware of the organization's existence. As a result scientists in other disciplines are not familiar with the research work published in the P.A.'s professional publications.

So the circle of confusion endlessly feeds upon itself. Funding isn't available. Few schools are providing the new recruits needed as researchers and educators in the field. Research results aren't communicated effectively to the public. There is little public pressure for psi research. So funding isn't made available. And so it goes.

But we believe the cycle can be broken. If reliable information is made available, sensationalism may become less of a problem. To that end, we think a psi information center should be established to help people get creditable and authoritative answers to their questions. We urge the P.A. or some other responsible professional organization to give leadership in stimulating interdisciplinary research and discussion, establishing accredited courses of study, and patrolling the false claims of "authorities" and spurious "news." We also hope psi researchers and researchers in other fields will talk to one another more and make an attempt to extend their investigations systematically.

Practicing psychics and healers might consider creating a code of ethics for themselves. Members of the media, because they have such enormous power to educate the public, might make a greater effort to familiarize themselves with research results and attempt to locate and use more reliable sources for information and comments on psi-related material. Lay interest groups might try to help their members better distinguish proven facts from speculation. Major foundations could play a vital role by helping to fund further research.

We hope that everyone will consider looking at psi in a fair and unbiased way. We urge people not to fall into the category of skeptics or that of believers, but simply to be curious, open minded, and willing to look at the facts as they become available.

Like Franklin's electricity, psi may be awaiting its Edison. But even now we have clues that its possible significance for our lives could be enormous. We have seen that human response to psi apparently occurs at an unconscious level. Could it be that we are all influencing one another all of the time without even being aware of doing so? Are we on the verge of proving scientifically how interconnected we are as human beings? How influential we are in each other's lives?

Expressed this way, it does not sound far-fetched, yet the implications are awesome. In pondering the possibilities of psi we see so clearly the significance of what it could mean for all of us to be co-creators in this unfinished universe. What a joyous thing it is to participate in the wonder of existence. And what a responsibility.

Resources

Guidelines
to Objectivity:
A Consumer's
Guide to Psi

In the course of evaluating the psi field, we have learned a number of things to watch out for. We have also developed a number of useful common-sense questions to ask.

Psychic Experiences
What if you have a psychic experience? What if you have a dream that comes true, an apparent telepathic communication, a possible poltergeist occurrence? Write down what happened, putting in as much detail as possible. If there are other people involved, ask them to write down their observations also. This is extremely important, because as one thinks and talks about psi events they tend to be changed, embroidered, and modified. A written record is invaluable.

Look at all possible explanations. If it is a case of precognition, ask in what other ways you might have received information or clues about what later took place. Could you simply have guessed that it might be going to happen? In instances of possible telepathy or clairvoyance, look for subtle clues that might have led you (consciously or unconsciously) to the information.

If the event involves PK—with the movement of objects or other physical effects—then look for natural causes. Could an accident have caused the event? Is it a misinterpretation of a normal event? Could a prankster be responsible?

Even if natural causes are eliminated, one cannot be certain that psi was at work, first because there may be an explanation that is yet to come, and secondly, because coincidences do occur.

What if others tell you of a psi experience that they or someone else had? As one might expect, the more second-hand or third-hand the experience, the more likely that the facts suffer from omissions, additions, and other distortions. Be alert to the mental state of people describing their own "psychic experiences" to you. Certain practices can generate hallucinations or other imaginary phenomena. These are very real to the person experiencing them but often have no relationship to external reality. Psi, on the contrary, is always concerned with a reality. It is a communication

141

between *two* people or between a person *and* a thing. Something that happens inside just one person's head is not objective evidence of psi.

When people tell you about a psychic experience, consider these questions.

Are they describing each detail carefully and completely?

Did any corroborative external occurrence take place?

Was the experience written down or recorded in some way?

Are there others who can describe the occurrence? What are their observations?

What other causes or explanations are there for the event—other than psi?

How much do the tellers of the experience want listeners to believe in it as a case of psi? Are they open to other explanations?

Psychics

Because psi is unpredictable, psychic information can be vague and is rarely completely accurate; even legitimate psychics are sometimes tempted to use subterfuge in order to be right all the time. Many means of deception are available.

Psychic phenomena are easy to simulate. Throughout the history of psi research, parapsychologists have uncovered ingenious tricks that create the illusion of psi. For example:

Telepathy. A standard trick of professional "mind readers" is to find something hidden somewhere in the audience. They select a member of the audience and tell him or her to concentrate on the location of the hidden object while they hold on to the person's wrist. The mind readers then appear to lead the person to the object. They do this by feeling the person's wrist muscles tense whenever they go in the wrong direction or overshoot the mark.

The ability to predict the future. Some mentalists send a sealed envelope to the mayor in a town where they are scheduled to appear. The envelope is said to contain the mentalist's prediction of the headline a local newspaper will carry on the day of the mentalist's performance, scheduled several days after the envelope was mailed. On stage during the performance, the mentalist slits the envelope with a trick letter opener that ejects the day's headline (which was written that morning on a small slip of paper) into the envelope. The astonished mayor then pulls it out and reads it.

Information from the Media

There is no way to be certain that trickery has not been used when supposedly psychic information is presented on film or tape. None of the books claiming to teach people how to have more ESP have been approved by a group of leading psi scientists. Few radio stations that claim expertise in psychic matters have boards of experts to advise them on the reliability of their material. Few TV or radio interviewers specializing in dealing with psychic phenomena have made their psychic credentials public.

As you try to separate the fact from the fiction, ask:

Where did the information come from?

Why should it be considered accurate?

What assurance is there that sources quoted are reliable?

When "experts say"—who are these experts? What is their basis of authority? Are they associated with a legitimate psi laboratory?

When it is said that "thorough research" has been done, exactly what does that mean? What experiments were conducted and how?

Has there been an advisory committee to assist in evaluating the information being passed on to the public? If so, who are its members? What are their credentials?

Ask "psychic interviewers" what their credentials are. What criteria do they use to evaluate information?

Ask any "psychic radio station" what experts advise it on the reliability of its information.

Authorities on Psi

There are so many self-proclaimed authorities in the field that it is difficult to distinguish between a real expert and a person who simply claims to be one. When considering teachers, course leaders, lecturers, or other self-described authorities on psi, remember that being an expert in another field doesn't automatically make one an expert in psi.

Knowledgeable teachers of psi do not offer broad generalizations about the subject. They advise students that no theory about what psi is or how it operates has yet been proven by psi researchers. They do not accept everything that is popularly supposed to involve psi. They do not rely heavily on reported spontaneous psychic experiences, but instead turn to the results of legitimate scientific research.

No method that claims to teach people how to use psi in daily life has yet been adequately tested by careful research. It takes more than a deck of cards or a pair of dice to be a controlled test of psi. Not all so-called scientific research really is scientific. Only a handful of centers exist in the entire world where subjects can be psi–tested and feel sure about the validity of the research. (See Appendix A for a list of some of these centers.)

Ask a self-described psi authority:

Is this information based on published research documentation or on popular books, personal experiences, and/or beliefs?

Do people agree or disagree with this opinion about psi? If so, who are they?

Is the authority a member of the Parapsychological Association?

Has he or she ever had anything published in a professional journal?

Ask psi researchers (in addition to the above questions):

Is there any other possible explanation for the psychic phenomena they say they have uncovered in their research?

Has their research been duplicated by anyone else? If so, who and where?

Will they report on the results of their research and submit that report to a professional journal for publication?

Consider these questions:

Do the psychics warn people that they are not correct all of the time?

What is their personal code of ethics regarding the use of psychic power? Do they exploit it? Do they practice for money?

Have they participated in any scientific experiments that were reported in professional journals? If so, where and when? Who conducted the experiments?

Are they willing to submit to scientific experiments conducted by outside researchers?

Ask "psychic healers" in addition to the questions listed above:

Do they recommend an orthodox medical check-up before treatment?

Do they recommend that people remain under the care of their physician, even though they are treating them?

Should patients continue taking medication their doctor has prescribed?

If a person being treated must be hospitalized, will the healers be able to comply with hospital regulations?

Psi Interest Groups

A number of groups of lay people are interested in psychic phenomena. Sometimes these interest groups focus on reported spontaneous psychic occurrences and not on published scientific experiments. Sometimes they provide forums for the presentation of commercial "psi products," which members are then encouraged to purchase.

Before you decide to join one of these groups, ask a spokesperson for the group such questions as:

What is the basic purpose of the group?

Is it solely interested in factual information about psychic phenomena?

What are its criteria for selecting speakers, programs, and resources?

How discriminating is it in evaluating information about psi?

Does it have an ethics committee that monitors information and makes sure factual presentations are absolutely accurate? If so, what are the qualifications of the members of this committee?

Do the members of the education and research committees read professional journals and report on them to the group?

Suggested Reading List

The following books have been suggested by the Psi SEARCH advisors.

Technical Bibliography

Beloff, J. (ed.) *New Directions in Parapsychology.* London: Elek, 1974.

Ciba Foundation. *Extrasensory Perception: A CIBA Foundation Symposium* (G. E. W. Wolstenholme and E. C. P. Millar, eds.) New York: Citadel, 1966 (paperback). Originally published by Little, Brown in 1956.

Eisenbud, J. *Psi and Psychoanalysis: Studies in the Psychoanalysis of Psi-Conditioned Behavior.* New York: Grune and Stratton, 1970.

Gauld, A. *The Founders of Psychical Research.* New York: Schocken, 1968.

Hansel, C. E. M. *ESP: A Scientific Evaluation.* New York: Scribner's, 1966 (hardcover and paperback).

Koestler, A. *The Roots of Coincidence.* New York: Random House, 1972.

Mitchell, E. D. *Psychic Exploration: A Challenge for Science* (J. White, ed.) New York: Putnam's, 1974.

Murphy, G. with Dale, L.A., *Challenge of Psychical Research: A Primer of Parapsychology.* New York: Harper & Row, 1961 (hardcover and paperback).

Podmore, F. *Mediums of the 19th Century.* 2 vols. New Hyde Park, N.Y.: University Books, 1963. Originally published by Methuen in 1902 as *Modern Spiritualism.*

Pratt, J. G. *Parapsychology: An Insider's View of ESP.* New York: Dutton, 1966.

Proceedings of an International Conference on Hypnosis, Drugs, Dreams, and Psi: Psi and Altered States of Consciousness. (R. Cavanna and M. Ullman, eds.) New York: Parapsychology Foundation, 1968 (available only from the foundation).

Proceedings of an International Conference on Methodology in Psi Research: Psi Favorable States of Consciousness. (R. Cavanna, ed.) New York: Parapsychology Foundation, 1970 (available only from the foundation).

Randall, J. *Parapsychology and the Nature of Life.* New York: Harper & Row, 1975.

Rao, K. R. *Experimental Parapsychology: A Review and Interpreta-*

tion, With a Comprehensive Bibliography. Springfield, Ill.: Thomas, 1966.

Rhine, J. B. and Pratt, J. G. *Parapsychology: Frontier Science of the Mind*, 2nd ed. Springfield, Ill.: Thomas, 1962.

Rhine, J. B. et al. *Extrasensory Perception After Sixty Years: A Critical Appraisal of the Research in Extrasensory Perception.* Boston: Bruce Humphries, 1966. Originally published by Holt in 1940.

Ryzl, M. *Parapsychology: A Scientific Approach.* New York: Hawthorn, 1970.

Schmeidler, G. (ed.) *Extrasensory Perception.* New York: Atherton, 1969 (hardcover and paperback).

Schmeidler, G. (ed.) *Parapsychology: Its Relation to Physics, Biology, Psychology, and Psychiatry.* Metuchen, N.J.: Scarecrow, 1976.

Smythies, J. R. (ed.) *Science and ESP.* New York: Humanities, 1967.

Soal, S. G. and Bateman, F. *Modern Experiments in Telepathy.* New Haven, Conn.: Yale University Press, 1954.

Thouless, R. H. *From Anecdote to Experiment in Psychical Research.* London: Routledge and Kegan Paul, 1972.

Tyrrell, G. N. M. *Apparitions.* New York: Macmillan, 1962 (paperback). Originally published by Duckworth in 1942.

Tyrrell, G. N. M. *Science and Psychical Phenomena.* New York: Harper & Brothers, 1938.

Ullman, M. and Krippner, S. *Dream Studies and Telepathy: An Experimental Approach.* New York: Parapsychology Foundation, 1970 (paperback; available only from the foundation).

Van Over, R. (ed.) *Psychology and Extrasensory Perception.* New York: New American Library, 1972 (paperback).

Vasiliev, L. L. *Experiments in Distant Influence.* New York: Dutton, 1976 (paperback).

White, R. A. *Surveys in Parapsychology.* Metuchen, N.J.: Scarecrow, 1976.

White, R. A. and Dale, L. A. *Parapsychology: Sources of Information.* Metuchen, N.J.: Scarecrow, 1973.

Wohlman, Benjamin, *Handbook of Parapsychology.* New York: Van Nostrand Reinhold, 1977.

Popular Bibliography

Ashby, R. H. *The Guide Book for the Study of Psychical Research.* New York: Weiser, 1972.

Christopher, M. *ESP, Seers and Psychics.* New York: Crowell, 1970.

Dean, E. D., Mihalasky, J., Ostrander, S., and Schroeder, L. *Executive ESP.* New York: Prentice-Hall, 1974.

Ebon, M. (ed.) *Test Your ESP.* New York: New American Library, 1971 (paperback). Originally published by World in 1970.

Eisenbud, J. *The World of Ted Serios: "Thoughtographic" Studies of an Extraordinary Mind*. New York: Paperback Library, 1969 (paperback). Originally published by Morrow in 1967.

Garrett, E. J. *Many Voices: The Autobiography of a Medium*. New York: Dell, 1969 (paperback). Originally published by Putnam in 1968.

Heywood, R. *The Sixth Sense: An Inquiry Into Extrasensory Perception*. London: Pan Books, 1971 (paperback). Originally published by Dutton in 1961 as *Beyond the Reach of Sense*.

LeShan, L. *The Medium, the Mystic and the Physicist: Toward a General Theory of the Paranormal*. New York: Viking, 1974.

McConnell, R. A. *ESP Curriculum Guide*. New York: Simon and Schuster, 1971 (hardcover and paperback).

Myers, F. W. H. *Human Personality and its Survival of Bodily Death*. (Abridged and edited by S. Smith.) New Hyde Park, N.Y.: University Books, 1961. Originally published in two volumes by Longmans, Green in 1903.

Owen, A. R. G. *Can We Explain the Poltergeist?* New York: Garrett/Helix, 1964.

Owen, A. R. G. and Sims, V. *Science and the Spook*. New York: Garrett, 1970.

Panati, C. *Supersenses*. New York: Doubleday, 1976 (paperback).

Pollack, J. *Croiset the Clairvoyant*. New York: Bantam, 1965 (paperback). Originally published by Doubleday in 1964.

Pratt, J. E. *ESP Research Today: A Study of Developments in Parapsychology Since 1960*. Metuchen, N. J.: Scarecrow, 1973.

Rawcliffe, D. H. *Occult and Supernatural Phenomena*. New York: Dover, 1971 (paperback). Originally published by Ridgway in 1952 as *The Psychology of the Occult*.

Rhine, J. B. *The Reach of the Mind*. New York: Peter Smith, 1972. New York: Morrow, 1971 (paperback). Originally published by Sloane in 1947.

Rhine, L. E. *ESP in Life and Lab: Tracing Hidden Channels*. New York: Macmillan, 1967 (hardcover and paperback).

Rhine, L. E. *Hidden Channels of the Mind*. New York: Sloane, 1961.

Rhine, L. E. *Mind Over Matter: Psychokinesis*. New York: Macmillan, 1970 (hardcover and paperback).

Rogo, D. S. *In Search of the Unknown*. New York: Taplinger, 1976.

Roll, W. G. *The Poltergeist*. New York: New American Library, 1972 (paperback).

Sinclair, U. *Mental Radio*. Springfield, Ill.: Thomas, 1962. Originally published by the author in 1930.

Ullman, M., Krippner, S., and Vaughan, A. *Dream Telepathy*. New York: Macmillan, 1973.

Vasiliev, L. *Mysterious Phenomena of the Human Psyche*. New Hyde Park, N.Y.: University Books, 1965.

Vaughan, A. *Patterns of Prophecy*. New York: Hawthorn, 1973.

West, D. J. *Psychical Research Today*. New York: Hillary, 1956 (paperback). Originally published by Duckworth in 1954.

Appendices

Centers of Parapsychological Research in the United States

This is a complete list of major psi laboratories and other institutions in which parapsychological research is done in the United States. Principal investigators at all of these places are members of the Parapsychological Association.

Psi Laboratories

Chester E. Carlson Research Laboratory
American Society for Psychical Research
5 West 73rd Street
New York, NY 10023

Center for Parapsychological Research
P.O. Box 5591
Austin, TX 78763

Institute for Parapsychology
Foundation for the Research on the Nature of Man
P.O. Box 6847, Duke Station
Durham, NC 27708

Division of Parapsychology and Psychophysics
Department of Psychiatry
Maimonides Medical Center
4802–10th Street
Brooklyn, NY 11219

Mind Science Foundation
102 West Rector, #209
San Antonio, TX 78216

Psychical Research Foundation
Duke Station
Durham, NC 27706

Psi researchers may also be found at:

Department of Psychology
City College of the City of New York
New York, NY 10010

Psi Communications Project
Newark College of Engineering
323 High Street
Newark, NJ 07102

Parapsychology Laboratory
Saint Joseph's College
54th Street and City Line
Philadelphia, PA 19131

Department of Psychology
University of California
Davis, CA 95616

Radiation Field Photography Laboratory
Neuropsychiatric Institute
University of California
Los Angeles, CA 90024

Tutorial Program
University of California
Santa Barbara, CA 93106

Division of Parapsychology
Department of Psychiatry
University of Virginia Medical School
Charlottesville, VA 22904

Electronics and Bioengineering Laboratory
Stanford Research Institute
333 Ravenswood Avenue
Menlo Park, CA 94025

Major English-Language Parapsychological Publications and Other Sources of Information about Psi

The major English-language scientific publications that publish research in the field of parapsychology and are affiliated with the Parapsychological Association are:

European Journal of Parapsychology (EJP)
Parapsychology Laboratory
University of Utrecht
Varkenmarkt 2
Utrecht 2501, The Netherlands

International Journal of Parapsychology (IJP)
Published between 1959 and 1968. Back issues may
   be obtained from:
Parapsychology Foundation
29 W. 57th Street
New York, NY 10019

Journal of Parapsychology (JP)
Foundation for Research on the Nature of Man
Box 6847, College Station
Durham, NC 27708

Journal of the American Society for Psychical Research (JASPR)
5 West 73rd Street
New York, NY 10023

Journal of the Society for Psychical Research (JSPR)
1 Adam and Eve Mews
Kensington, London W86UQ, England

Research in Parapsychology (RIP)
Reports of the briefs presented at the annual meetings of the
Parapsychological Association
P.O. Box 7503
Alexandria, VA 22307

Other Sources of Information

American Society of Psychical Research
5 West 73rd Street
New York, NY 10023

Central Premonitions Registry
Box 482 Times Square Station
New York, NY 10036

Council of Nurse-Healers
33 Ora Way
San Francisco, CA 94131

Parapsychology Foundation
29 West 57th Street
New York, NY 10019

The Parapsychological Association
P.O. Box 7503
Alexandria, VA 22307

Glossary

AGENT   The person who is the sender in a telepathy experiment, or who seems to be the source of spontaneous psi effects. See RSPK AGENT

ALPHA WAVES (OR ALPHA RHYTHM)   A mode of electrical activity detectable on the surface of the brain, with frequencies of about eight to twelve waves per second, that generally predominates when an individual is in a quiet waking state or in meditation.

ALTERED STATE OF CONSCIOUSNESS (ASC)   A mental condition in which modes of perception and mental functioning are qualitatively different from those of the normal waking state.

ANPSI   Psi phenomena in which animals are involved.

APPARITION   A realistic visual hallucination, usually of a person, which in many cases involves paranormal communication. See HALLUCINATION.

ASC   See ALTERED STATE OF CONSCIOUSNESS.

AURA   A luminous form that some psychics claim to see around a person's body; the shape and color of the aura are supposedly related to the person's health and emotional state.

AUTOMATIC WRITING   Writing done while the writer is in a dissociated state and unconscious of the writing.

AUTOMATISM   Any normally conscious activity that is carried out in a dissociated state without conscious awareness or direction.

BARRIER   Any means used in a psi experiment to prevent the person being tested from knowing or influencing the target by normal means.

BIOFEEDBACK   A technique by which one may learn to control an unconscious bodily function, such as heart rate, by observing information fed back by an instrument that is monitoring the function.

CHANCE   The result that would be expected, over the long run, according to the laws of probability, in the absence of any systematic influence.

CLAIRVOYANCE   Extrasensory perception of objects or events. Formerly ESP via visual impression.

CONSCIOUSNESS   A state of awareness of things and conditions as a whole in the environment.

CONTROL   The personality, ostensibly a disembodied spirit, that regularly displaces the normal personality of a trance medium and mediates between sitters and spirit communicators. See MEDIUM, TRANCE.

DECLINE EFFECT   In psi experiments, the tendency for scores to decline during a series of trials.

DEVIATION   In a psi test, the difference between the actual score and that to be expected by chance (the mean chance expectation).

DISCARNATE   Existing apart from a physical body, a condition attributed to spirits of the dead and some other entities.

DISSOCIATION   A state of mental organization in which one carries on certain activities unconsciously or in the awareness of a secondary personality. See AUTOMATISM.

DOWSING   Searching for something hidden, generally underground, by noticing movements of a forked stick or other hand-held device held over the place of concealment. See AUTOMATISM.

ESP   See EXTRASENSORY PERCEPTION.

ESP CARDS   (Also known as ZENER CARDS.) Cards designed for use as targets in ESP tests. Each has one of five symbols (star, circle, cross, square, and wavy lines). A deck consists of twenty-five cards, five of each symbol.

EXTRASENSORY PERCEPTION (ESP)   The obtaining of information that is not accessible by means of any known sense.

FORCED-CHOICE TEST   An ESP test in which the subject must choose one of a limited number of prescribed targets, such as ESP card symbols.

FREE-RESPONSE TEST   An ESP test in which subjects respond to a picture or other complex target with whatever imagery or feeling they believe relates to the target.

GANZFELD   (German: *entire field*) An experimental situation in which a subject is exposed to uniform sensory stimulation without accompanying information: for example, by using translucent eye screens, random noise in earphones, and so forth.

GENERAL EXTRASENSORY PERCEPTION (GESP)   A psi test mode in which no attempt is made to distinguish between telepathy and clairvoyance.

GHOST   Apparition of nonliving individual. See AP-PARITION

HALLUCINATION   The apparent realistic experiencing of sensations without any physical basis for the sensations.

HAUNTING   A paranormal phenomenon that is manifested repeatedly at a particular place, usually a house.

HIT   In a psi test, a successful trial. See TRIAL.

ILLUSION   A misinterpretation of sensory information.

INTUITION   Subjective conviction or insight attained without conscious justification.

KIRLIAN PHOTOGRAPHY   A method of recording the electric field pattern around an object placed in the field near a photographic film.

LEVITATION   Alleged lifting or elevation of an object without known physical means.

MEDIUM   A psychic who communicates information and sometimes produces physical effects ostensibly by the agency of discarnate spirits.

MESMERISM   A school of thought popular in the eighteenth and nineteenth centuries that attributed unexplained cures, trance states, and paranormal phenomena to "animal magnetism," an invisible fluid in the body.

MISS   In a psi test, an unsuccessful trial.

MYSTICISM   A system of belief that relies upon certain intuitive experiences for spiritual development and insight into the nature of the world.

OUT-OF-BODY EXPERIENCE (OBE or OOBE)   An experience in which people feel that they are seeing the world from some specific place outside their physical bodies.

PARANORMAL   Beyond understanding in terms of known causes and processes.

PARAPSYCHOLOGY   The scientific study of situations in which a human or other organism acquires information from its environment or exerts physical influence upon it independently of its senses or motor mechanisms.

PK   See PSYCHOKINESIS.

PLETHYSMOGRAPH   A device to monitor changes in the amount of blood flowing through the vessels near the skin.

PMIR   See PSI-MEDIATED INSTRUMENTAL RESPONSE.

POLTERGEIST PHENOMENA   (German: noisy ghost) Spontaneously occurring paranormal sounds, movements of objects, and other effects, usually in the vicinity of a specific person.

POSSESSION   A condition suggesting that a person's mind has been taken over by an alien personality, usually believed to be a discarnate spirit.

PRECOGNITION   Extrasensory perception of future events. See EXTRASENSORY PERCEPTION.

PROBABILITY OF SUCCESS   The degree of likelihood that a possible event will occur, expressed in mathematical terms—usually a decimal fraction: $p < .01$ = odds of 100 to 1 or less.

PSI   A term used by parapsychologists to refer to the unknown factor(s) responsible for those interactions between organisms and their environments that do not appear to conform to the known laws of science; the subject matter of parapsychology. See PARAPSYCHOLOGY.

PSI-MEDIATED INSTRUMENTAL RESPONSE (PMIR)   A technical term for the presumed unconscious use of psi abilities in everyday situations to help one achieve one's purposes or even to gain benefits of which one is not aware.

PSI MISSING   In a psi test, scoring significantly lower than should be expected by chance.

PSYCHIC   Pertaining to psi; also, someone who shows evidence of exceptional psi ability.

PSYCHICAL RESEARCH   An earlier name for parapsychology. See PARAPSYCHOLOGY.

PSYCHIC HEALING   Healing by laying-on-of-hands, directed mental activity, or other paranormal means.

PSYCHIC SURGERY   Alleged paranormal cutting and healing of incisions to remove or repair abnormal tissue.

PSYCHOKINESIS (PK)   Paranormal influence upon a physical object or situation by mental effort or intention.

PSYCHOPHOTOGRAPHY   The production of images on photographic film by mental effort.

RANDOM EVENT   An event that cannot be predicted from observations of preceding events.

RAPID EYE MOVEMENT (REM)   Characteristic eye movements that occur when a person is dreaming.

RECEIVER   In a telepathy test, the person who is trying to obtain information that is in the mind of the sender.

RECURRENT SPONTANEOUS PSYCHOKINESIS (RSPK)   A technical term for poltergeist phenomena. See POLTERGEIST.

REINCARNATION   The doctrine that some element of a personality survives death and is reborn in the body of an infant.

REM   See RAPID EYE MOVEMENT.

REMOTE VIEWING   An ESP test procedure in which the subject tries to see a randomly selected distant place to which the sender has gone.

RSPK   See RECURRENT SPONTANEOUS PSYCHOKINESIS

RSPK AGENT   Any person whose presence appears to be necessary for the RSPK phenomena to occur. See POLTERGEIST.

RUN   A group of consecutive psi test trials done without interruption or change of procedure.

SCORE   In a psi test, the number of hits in a run or other unit.

SÉANCE   Literally, a sitting. A meeting of several people, usually with a medium, for spirit communication or the production of psychokinetic effects.

SENDER   In a telepathy test, the person who is trying

to send information to the subject.

SENSITIVE   Someone who shows evidence of exceptional psi ability, particularly in ESP; a psychic.

SENSORY DEPRIVATION   For experimental purposes, subjecting people to monotonous, informationless sensory stimulation, or depriving them of practically all sensory inputs. See GANZFELD.

SERIES   In a psi experiment, a succession of runs done under uniform conditions.

SIGNIFICANCE   In statistics, a loosely defined term expressing the degree of confidence that the outcome of a given study is not due to chance. For example, if the probability that an observed psi test score is due to chance influences is 1 in 5, the score obviously is of no significance as evidence of psi; but if the probability is 1 in 1,000, chance becomes an unlikely explanation, and the result is regarded as highly significant. Parapsychologists generally consider a result significant if its probability of occurrence by chance is 1 in 100 or less. See PROBABILITY OF SUCCESS.

SPIRITUALISM   A religion based upon the belief that spirits of the dead can communicate with the living through psychically sensitive people called mediums.

SUBJECT   The person who is being tested in an experiment.

SURVIVAL   The supposed persistence after bodily death of an identifiable remnant or aspect of a pesonality.

TARGET   The aspect of the environment toward which subjects are asked to direct their psi ability in an experiment.

TAROT CARDS   A deck of cards, believed to be derived from ancient Egypt, that is used for fortune telling.

TELEPATHY   Extrasensory perception of information that exists only in the mind of another person.

TRANCE   An altered state of consciousness, self-induced or induced by hypnosis or other means, that involves modification or cessation of normal consciousness and emergence of ordinarily inaccessible mental information or processes.

TRIAL   A single attempt by a subject to use psi ability in an experiment.

ZENER CARDS   Cards named for their designer Karl Zener. See *ESP CARDS*.

Notes

2. Obstacles to Objectivity

1. G. N. M. Tyrrell, *Science and Psychical Phenomena* (New York: Harper Brothers, 1938), p. 341.

2. S. Holroyd, *Psi and the Consciousness Explosion* (New York: Taplinger, 1977), p. 129.

3. D. S. Rogo, *Parapsychology: A Century of Inquiry* (New York: Taplinger, 1975), p. 19.

4. Upton Sinclair, *Mental Radio* (New York: Boni, 1920), p. 172.

5. D. J. West, "The Strengths and Weakness of the Available Evidence for Extrasensory Perception," in G. E. W. Wolstenholme and E. Millar, *CIBA Foundation Symposium on Extrasensory Perception* (New York: Citadel, 1966), pp. 20–21.

6. Tyrrell, *Science and Psychical Phenomena*, p. 117.

7. G. Murphy, "Trends in the Study of Extrasensory Perception," *American Psychologist*, 13 (1958): 69–77.

3. Inside Laboratory Walls

1. C. Honorton and S. Harper, "Psi-mediated Imagery and Ideation in an Experimental Procedure for Regulating Perceptual Input," *JASPR*, 68 (1974): 156–168.

2. E. Messer, personal communication with the authors, summer 1976.

3. J. B. Rhine et al., *Extrasensory Perception After Sixty Years: A Critical Appraisal of the Research in Extrasensory Perception* (Boston: Bruce Humphries, 1966; originally published by Holt in 1940), p. 191.

4. C. Honorton, "Psi and Internal Attention States: Information Retrieval in the Ganzfeld," *Proceedings of the Parapsychological Foundation, Paris 1977* (New York: The Parapsychological Foundation, in press).

5. M. Crichton, *Eaters of the Dead* (New York: Knopf, 1976), p. 187.

6. R. H. Thouless, *From Anecdote to Experiment in Psychical Research* (London: Routledge and Kegan Paul, 1972), p. 53.

4. Psi Exists

1. Psi SEARCH Exhibit.

2. C. Tart, in *The New Yorker*, December 13, 1976, p. 38.

3. H. von Helmholtz, Speech to the British Association of Physicists, circa 1880.

4. D. O. Hebb, "The Role of Neurological Ideas in Psychology," *Journal of Personality*, XX (1951): 45.

5. C. E. M. Hansel, *ESP: A Scientific Evaluation* (New York: Scribner's, 1966), p. 241.

6. K. R. Rao, *Experimental Parapsychology* (Springfield, Ill.: Thomas, 1966), p. 140.

7. J. B. Rhine, *Extra-Sensory Perception* (Boston: Humphries, 1935; originally published in 1934 in the *Proceedings of the Boston Society for Psychic Research*).

8. J. B. Rhine, personal communication with the authors, March 25, 1977.

9. J. B. Rhine, *Extra-Sensory Perception*.

10. C. Honorton, personal communication with the authors, December 2, 1976.

11. C. E. M. Hansel, *ESP*.

12. J. B. Rhine, *Extra-Sensory Perception*.

13. C. Honorton, "Error Some Place!" *Journal of Communication*, 25 (Winter 1975): 105–107.

14. J. B. Rhine et al., *Extrasensory Perception After Sixty Years: A Critical Appraisal of the Research in Extrasensory Perception* (Boston: Humphries, 1966; originally published by Holt in 1940), p. 191.

15. Honorton, "Error Some Place!" p. 107.

16. J. B. Rhine, March 25, 1977.

17. L. E. Rhine and J. B. Rhine, "The Psychokinetic Effect: I. The First Experiment," *Journal of Parapsychology*, 7, 1 (1943): 20–43.

18. J. B. Rhine, March 25, 1977.

19. J. B. Rhine, March 25, 1977.

20. H. Schmidt, personal communication with the authors, March 19, 1977.

21. H. Schmidt, "A PK Test with Electronic Equipment," *Journal of Parapsychology*, 34 (1970): 175–181.

22. For a complete list, see J. D. Morris et al. (eds.), *Research in Parapsychology 1975* (Metuchen, N.J.: Scarecrow, 1977), p. 214.

23. Schmidt, March 19, 1977.

24. L. Braud and W. Braud, "The Psi Conducive Syndrome: Free Response GESP Performance During an Experimental Hypnagogic State Induced by Visual and Acoustic Ganzfeld Techniques," in J. D. Morris et al. (eds.), *Research in Parapsychology 1974* (Metuchen, N.J.: Scarecrow, 1975): 20–23.

25. M. York, "The Defense Mechanism Test (DMT) as an Indicator of Psychic Performance as Measured by a Free Response Clairvoyance Task Using a Ganzfeld Technique," in J. D. Morris et al. (eds.), *Research in Parapsychology 1976* (Metuchen, N.J.: Scarecrow, 1977): 48–49.

26. R. Stanford and A. Neylon, "Experiential Factors Related to Free-Response Clairvoyance Performance in a Sensory Uniformity Setting," *Research in Parapsychology 1974* (Metuchen, N.J.: Scarecrow, 1975): 89–96.

27. C. Honorton, "Psi and Internal Attention States: Information Retrieval in the Ganzfeld," *Proceedings of the Parapsychological Foundation, Paris 1977* (New York: The Parapsychological Foundation, in press).

28. W. G. Roll and J. Klein, "Further Forced-Choice ESP Experiments with Lalsingh Harribance," *JASPR*, 66, 1 (January 1972): 103–112.

29. L. Harribance and R. Neff, *This Man Knows You* (Naylor Press, 1975).

30. W. G. Roll, personal communication with the authors, April 7, 1977.

31. W. G. Roll, personal communication with the authors, March 19, 1977.

32. Hansel, *ESP*, pp. 59–60.

33. Rao, *Experimental Parapsychology*, p. 91.

34. M. Mead, Introduction to R. Targ and H. Puthoff, *Mind Reach* (New York: Delacorte, 1977), p. xvi.

35. G. Murphy, *Challenge of Psychical Research* (New York: Harper & Row, 1970), p. 81.

5. Who Can Use Psi?

1. G. Murphy, "Psychical Research and Personality," *JASPR*, 44 (1950): 5.

2. C. Tart, in *The New Yorker*, December 13, 1976, p. 37

3. Tart, *The New Yorker*, p. 38.

4. Psi SEARCH Exhibit.

5. Psi SEARCH.

6. C. Honorton and S. Harper, "Psi-Mediated Imagery and Ideation in an Experimental Procedure for Regulating Perceptual Input," *JASPR*, 68 (1974): 156–168.

7. L. E. Rhine and J. B. Rhine, "The Psychokinetic Effect: I. The First Experiment," *Journal of Parapsychology*, 7 (1943), 1: 27.

8. Rhine and Rhine, p. 27.

9. R. Brier, as reported in W. G. Roll (ed), *Proceedings of the Parapsychological Association*, 1966, no. 3: 27.

10. B. M. Humphrey, "ESP and Intelligence," *Journal of Parapsychology*, 9 (1945): 7–16.

11. M. Scriven, "The Frontiers of Psychology: Psychoanalysis and Parapsychology," in *Science and Philosophy* (Pittsburgh: University of Pittsburgh Press, 1962).

12. G. R. Schmeidler and R. A. McConnell, *ESP and Personality Patterns* (New Haven, Conn.: Yale University Press, 1958).

13. J. Palmer, "Scoring in ESP Tests as a Function of Belief in ESP, Part 1. The Sheep-Goat Effect," *JASPR*, 65 (1971): 373–407.

14. C. Honorton, L. Tierney, and D. Torres, "The Role of Mental Imagery in Psi-Mediation," *JASPR*, 68 (1974): 385–394.

15. C. Honorton, "Reported Frequency of Dream Recall and ESP," *JASPR*, 66 (1972): 369–374.

16. J. B. Rhine, "Psi-Missing Reexamined," *Journal of Parapsychology*, 33 (1969) : 1–38.

17. C. Tart, *Learning to Use Extrasensory Perception* (Chicago: University of Chicago Press, 1976), p. 76.

18. Tart, *The New Yorker*, p. 37.

19. R. Stanford, personal communication with the authors, April 4, 1977.

20. Tart, *The New Yorker*, p. 38.

21. Honorton and Harper, "Psi-Mediated Imagery."

22. G. Schmeidler, "PK Effects Upon Continuously Recorded Temperatures," *JASPR*, 67 (1973): 325–340.

23. G. Schmeidler, personal communication with the authors, May 15, 1977.

24. G. Schmeidler, "The Psychic Personality," in Mitchell, *Psychic Exploration* (New York: Putnam's, 1974), p. 94.

25. Schmeidler, "PK Effects."

26. Schmeidler, "PK Effects."

27. Schmeidler, May 15, 1977.

28. D. S. Rogo, *Parapsychology: A Century of Inquiry* (New York: Taplinger, 1975), p. 254.

29. Psi SEARCH Exhibit.

30. G. K. Watkins and A. Watkins, "Possible PK Influence on the Resuscitation of Anesthetized Mice," *Journal of Parapsychology*, 35 (1971): 257–272.

31. B. Grad, "Some Biological Effects of the 'Laying on of Hands': A Review of Experiments with Animals and Plants," *JASPR*, 59 (1965): 95–127.

32. J. B. Rhine and S. Feather, "The Study of Cases of Psi-Trailing in Animals," *Journal of Parapsychology*, 26 (1962): 1–22.

33. Rogo, *Parapsychology*, pp. 252–253. (This statement applied to a mixture of animal anecdotes and experimental reports.)

34. R. Morris, "The Use of Detectors for Out-of-Body Experiences," *Parapsychological Association Proceedings*, 1973, pp. 114–116.

35. R. Morris, personal communication with the authors, March 29, 1977.

36. R. Morris, "Parapsychology and Biology," in G. Schmeidler (ed.), *Parapsychology and Its Relation to Physics, Biology, Psychology and Psychiatry* (Metuchen, N.J.: Scarecrow, 1976), p. 64.

37. Morris, March 29, 1977.

38. S. B. Harary, personal communication with the authors, May 15, 1977.

39. J. B. von Helmont, *Opuscula Medica Inaudita* (1644).

6. What Can Psi Communicate?

1. K. R. Rao, *Experimental Parapsychology* (Springfield, Ill.: Thomas, 1966), p. 55.

2. R. Van de Castle, personal communication with the authors, April 7, 1977.

3. R. H. Thouless, *From Anecdote to Experiment in Psychical Research* (London: Routledge and Kegan Paul, 1972), p. 19.

4. L. E. Rhine and J. B. Rhine, "The Psychokinetic Effect: I. The First Experiment," *Journal of Parapsychology*, 7, 1 (March 1943).

5. W. Cox, "A Cumulative Assessment of PK on Multiple Targets," *Journal of Parapsychology*, 29 (1965): 299–30.

6. J. Eisenbud et al. "Two Camera and Television Experiments with Ted Serios," *JASPR*, 64 (1970): 261–276.

7. B. Grad, "Some Biological Effects of the 'Laying on of Hands': A Review of Experiments with Animals and Plants," *JASPR*, 59 (1965): 95–127.

8. K. Osis, "A Test of the Occurrence of a Psi Effect Between Man and Cat," *Journal of Parapsychology*, 16 (1952): 233–256.

9. J. Smith, "Paranormal Effects on Enzyme Activity," *Proceedings of the Parapsychological Association*, 5 (1968): 15–16.

10. W. Cox, "The Effect of PK on Electromechanical Systems," *Journal of Parapsychology*, 29 (1965): 165–175.

11. H. Schmidt, "A PK Test with Electronic Equipment," *Journal of Parapsychology*, 34 (1970): 175–181.

12. J. B. Rhine, *Extra-Sensory Perception* (Boston: Humphries, 1935; originally published in 1934 in the *Proceedings of the Boston Society for Psychic Research*).

13. J. A. Freeman and W. Nielsen, "Precognition Score Deviations as Related to Anxiety Levels," *Journal of Parapsychology*, 28 (1964): 239–249.

14. S. Krippner and M. Ullman, "Telepathy and Dreams: A Controlled Experiment with EEG–EOG Monitoring," *Journal of Nervous and Mental Disorders*, 151 (1970): 394–403.

15. J. Fahler and K. Osis, "Checking for Awareness of Hits in a Precognitive Experiment with Hypnotized Subjects," *JASPR*, 60, 4 (October 1966): 340–345.

16. R. Targ and H. Puthoff, "Information Transmission under Conditions of Sensory Shielding," *Nature*, 251 (October 18, 1974): 602–607.

17. E. D. Dean and C. B. Nash, "Coincident Plethysmograph Results Under Controlled Conditions," *Journal of the Society for Psychical Research*, 44, 731 (March 1967): 1–11.

18. W. G. Roll, R. L. Morris, J. A. Damgaard, J. Klein, and M. Roll, "Free Verbal Response Experiments with Lalsingh Harribance," *JASPR*, 67 (1973): 197–207.

19. G. Murphy, *Challenge of Psychical Research* (New York: Harper & Row, 1970), p. 67.

20. Thouless, *From Anecdote to Experiment*, p. 52.

21. G. K. Watkins and A. M. Watkins, "Apparent Psychokinesis on Static Objects by a 'Gifted' Subject: A Laboratory Demonstration," in W. G. Roll et al. (eds.), *Research in Parapsychology 1973* (Metuchen, N. J.: Scarecrow, 1974), pp. 132–134.

22. H. Puthoff and R. Targ, "PK Experiments with Uri Geller and Ingo Swann," in W. G. Roll et al. (eds.), *Research in Parapsychology 1973* (Metuchen, N. J.: Scarecrow, 1974), pp. 125–128.

23. G. K. Watkins and A. M. Watkins, "Possible PK Influence on the Resuscitation of Anesthetized Mice," *Journal of Parapsychology*, 35 (1971): 257–272.

24. D. Krieger, "Healing by the Laying on of Hands as a Facilitator of Bioenergetic Change. The Response of In-Vivo Human Hemoglobin," *Psychoenergetic Systems*, 3 (1975).

25. M. J. Smith, "Paranormal Effects on Enzyme Activity," *Proceedings of the Parapsychological Association*, 5 (1968): 15–16.

26. Grad, "Some Biological Effects."

27. J. B. Rhine, *New Frontiers of the Mind* (London: Faber and Faber, 1937).

28. R. Warcollier, *Experimental Telepathy* (Boston: Society for Psychical Research, 1938), p. 101.

29. R. Van de Castle, "Psi Abilities in Primitive Groups" (Presidential Address), *Proceedings of the Parapsychological Association*, 7 (1970): 97–122.

30. Van de Castle, "Psi Abilities."

31. T. Moss and J. A. Gengerelli, "Telepathy and Emotional Stimuli: A Controlled Experiment," *Journal of Abnormal Psychology*, 72 (1967): 341–348.

32. *Psi Lines: A Documentation of the Psi SEARCH Exhibition* (Los Angeles: Psi SEARCH Institute, 1975), p. 17

33. R. Van de Castle, personal communication with the authors, April 7, 1977.

34. Targ and Puthoff, "Information Transmission."

35. R. Targ and H. Puthoff, *Mind Reach* (New York: Delacorte, 1977), pp. 132–133.

36. Targ and Puthoff, *Mind Reach*, p. 134.

37. R. Stanford, "An Experimentally Testable Model for Spontaneous Psi Events: I. Extrasensory Events," *JASPR*, 68, 1 (January 1974): 34.

38. R. Stanford, personal communication with the authors, April 4, 1977.

7. When Does a Psi Exchange Occur?

1. D. S. Rogo, *Parapsychology: A Century of Inquiry* (New York: Taplinger, 1975), p. 283.

2. L. E. Rhine, *Hidden Channels of the Mind* (New York: Sloane, 1967), pp. 12–14.

3. G. Murphy, "Trends in the Study of Extrasensory Perception," *American Psychologist*, 13 (1958): 69–76.

4. C. Honorton, personal communication with the authors, November 27, 1976.

5. J. Fahler and K. Osis, "Checking for Awareness of Hits in a Precognitive Experiment with Hypnotized Subjects," *JASPR*, 60, 4 (October 1966): 340–345.

6. K. Osis, personal communication with the authors, April 12, 1977.

7. S. Krippner, M. Ullman, and C. Honorton, "A Precognitive Dream Study with a Single Subject," *JASPR*, 65, 2 (April 1971): 192–203.

8. Psi SEARCH Exhibit.

9. C. Honorton, personal communication with the authors, April 16, 1977.

10. R. Targ and H. Puthoff, "Information Transmission Under Conditions of Sensory Shielding," *Nature*, 251 (October 18, 1974): 602–604.

11. R. Targ and H. Puthoff, *Mind Reach* (New York: Delacorte, 1977), p. 4.

12. J. G. Pratt, *ESP Research Today: A Study of Developments in Parapsychology Since 1960* (Metuchen, N. J.: Scarecrow Press, 1973), p. 30.

13. L. Braud and W. Braud, "Further Studies of Relaxation as a Psi-Conducive State," *JASPR*, 68, 3 (1974): 229–245.

14. L. Braud and W. Braud, "Preliminary Explorations of Psi-Conducive State: Progressive Muscular Relaxation," *JASPR*, 67 (1973): 26–46.

15. Braud and Braud, "Preliminary Explorations."

16. Braud and Braud, "Further Studies."

17. Psi SEARCH Exhibit.

18. S. Freud, "Dreams and the Occult," in *New Introductory Lectures on Psychoanalysis* (London: Hogarth, 1934).

19. C. Honorton and S. Krippner, "Hypnosis and ESP Performance: A Review of the Experimental Literature," *JASPR*, 63 (1969): 214–252.

20. Pratt, *Parapsychology since 1960*, p. 31.

21. C. Honorton and S. Harper, "Psi-Mediated Imagery and Ideation in an Experimental Procedure for Regulating Perceptual Input," *JASPR*, 68 (1974): 156–168.

22. C. Honorton with C. Carbone, "A Preliminary Study of Feedback—Augmented EEG Alpha Activity and ESP Card Guessing Performance," *JASPR*, 65 (1971): 66–74.

23. Psi SEARCH Exhibit.

24. C. Tart, "A Psychophysiological Study of Out-of-Body Experiences in a Selected Subject," *JASPR*, 62, 1 (January 1968): 3–27.

25. C. Tart, "Some Methodological Problems in OOBE Research: Comments on the Symposium," in W. G. Roll et al. (eds.), *Research in Parapsychology 1973* (Metuchen, N. J.: Scarecrow, 1974), pp. 116–117.

26. Psi SEARCH Exhibit.

8. Where Can Psi Occur?

1. R. Warcollier, *Experiments in Telepathy* (New York: Harper Brothers, 1938).

2. Psi SEARCH Exhibit.

3. L. E. Rhine, *Hidden Channels of the Mind* (New York: Sloane, 1961), p. 145.

4. E. D. Dean and C. B. Nash, Coincident Plethysmograph Results under Controlled Conditions," *Journal of the Society for Psychical Research*, 44, 731 (March 1967): 1–11.

5. E. D. Dean, personal communication with the authors, April 8, 1977.

6. Dean, April 8, 1977.

7. E. Kelly, personal communication with the authors, April 19, 1977.

8. R. Targ and H. Puthoff, "Information Transmission Under Conditions of Sensory Shielding," *Nature*, 252 (Oc-

tober 18, 1974): 602–607.

9. J. Scanlon, *New Scientist* (October 1974): 181–185.

10. Psi SEARCH Exhibit.

11. J. B. Rhine, *Reach of the Mind* (New York: Sloane, 1947), p. 57.

12. M. Scriven, "The Frontiers of Psychology: Psychoanalysis and Parapsychology," in *Science and Philosophy* (Pittsburgh: University of Pittsburgh Press, 1962).

13. E. D. Dean, "Long Distance Plethysmograph Telepathy with Agent under Water," *Proceedings of the Parapsychological Association*, 6 (1969): 41–42.

14. Targ and Puthoff, "Information Transmission," pp. 602–607.

15. Targ and Puthoff, "Information Transmission," p. 605.

16. G. Schmeidler, "PK Effects Upon Continuously Recorded Temperatures," *JASPR*, 67 (1973): 325–340.

17. G. Murphy, *Challenge of Psychical Research* (New York: Harper & Row, 1970).

9. The How and Why of Psi

1. J. Beloff, "The Place of Theory in Parapsychology," in R. Van Over (ed.), *Psychology and Extrasensory Perception* (New York: Mentor, 1972), p. 379.

2. G. Murphy, *Challenge of Psychical Research* (New York: Harper & Row, 1970), p. 285.

3. M. Mead, Introduction to R. Targ and H. Puthoff, *Mind Reach* (New York: Delacorte, 1977), p. xix.

4. J. B. Rhine, letter to the authors, January 1977.

5. M. Johnson, Address at the University of North Carolina, Chapel Hill, North Carolina, April 23, 1976.

6. W. Braud, personal communication with the authors, April 11, 1977.

7. J. Eisenbud, "Why Psi?" *The Psychoanalytic Review*, 77 (Winter 1966): 153.

8. G. Murphy, "On Psychical Research," *Journal of Communications*, 25:1, (Winter, 1975): Annenberg School of Communications, p 102.

9. J. B. Rhine, *New Frontiers of the Mind* (New York: Farrar and Rinehart, 1937), p. 190.

10. M. Ryzl, *Parapsychology—a Scientific Approach* (New York: Hawthorn, 1970), p. 192.

10. Psi Beyond Laboratory Walls

1. W. G. Roll and J. G. Pratt, "The Miami Disturbances," *JASPR*, 65 (1971): 409–454; W. G. Roll et al., "Radial and Tangential Forces in the Miami Poltergeist," *JASPR*, 67 (1973): 267–281.

2. W. G. Roll, *The Poltergeist* (New York: New American Library, 1972).

3. J. G. Pratt, *ESP Research Today* (Metuchen, N. J.: Scarecrow, 1973).

4. As quoted in Roll, *The Poltergeist*, p. 114.

5. J. G. Pratt, personal communication with the authors, September 9, 1976.

6. H. Price, *Poltergeist over England* (London: Country Life Ltd., 1945), pp. 81–110.

7. For further information, see H. Harrington and N. Fodor, *Haunted People* (New York: Dutton, 1951); and A. R. G. Owen, *Can We Explain the Poltergeist?* (New York: Garrett/Helix, 1964).

8. H. Bender, "New Developments in Poltergeist Research" (Presidential Address), *Proceedings of the Parapsychological Association*, 6 (1969): 81–102.

9. Roll and Pratt, "The Miami Disturbances," p. 453.

11. Some Traditional Associations

1. *Preliminary Report of the Commission Appointed by the University of Pennsylvania to Investigate Modern Spiritualism* (Philadelphia: Lippincott, 1887).

2. See, for example, *Revelations of a Spirit Medium* (Reprinted and edited by E. Dingwall and H. Price, 1922); and *Confessions of a Medium* (London: Griffith, Farrar, Okeden and Walsh, n.d.)

3. For a survey of the origin of Spiritualism, see A. Gauld, *The Founders of Psychical Research* (New York: Schocken, 1968), pp. 3–31.

4. G. Murphy, "The Importance of Spontaneous Cases," *JASPR*, 47, 3 (July 1953): 93.

5. Murphy, "The Importance," p. 101.

6. D. J. West, "The Investigation of Spontaneous Cases," *Proceedings of the Society for Psychical Research*, 48 (1946–1949): 264–300.

7. M. Smith, *Journal of the Society for Psychical Research* (July 1895): 122.

8. Smith, p. 123.

9. Smith, p. 123.

10. West, "The Investigation," p. 291.

11. Letter from Grazina Babusis to Fran Hynds, December 4, 1976.

12. West, "The Investigation," p. 271.

13. For examples of such systematic studies, see G. Murphy, *Challenge of Psychical Research* (New York: Harper & Row, 1970), pp. 38–41, 44–49.

14. For further information, see E. R. Dodds, "Supernormal Phenomena in Classical Antiquity," *Proceedings of the Society for Psychical Research*, 55 (1971): 189–237; and P. Haining, *Ghosts: The Illustrated History* (New York: Macmillan, 1975).

15. "Mrs. Anna Nicolaienna Broussiloff to Mr. A. Aksakoff," *Journal of the Society for Psychical Research* (July 1895): 121

16. C. L. Tweedale, *Journal of the Society for Psychical Research* (November 1906): 323–324.

17. G. Grobicki, *JASPR*, 47, 3 (July 1953): 84–85.

18. R. Morton, "Record of a Haunted House," *Proceedings of the Society for Psychical Research*, 8 (1892): 311–332.

19. G. Schmeidler, "Quantitative Investigation of a Haunted House, *JASPR*, 60 (April 1966): 137–149. Smeidler investigated the reports of three family members in the New York area who said they had experienced a ghost. Schmeidler gave them a personality checklist, on which they rated the "ghost," and also a floor plan of the house, where they marked the places they frequently experienced the apparition. Nine sensitives were taken through the house by people unfamiliar with the case. The sensitives marked locations on the floor plan and filled in the personality checklist according to their experiences of the ghost. Two sensitives had significantly accurate results with the floor plan, and four others had significant correspondence with the family checklist. However, there were no controls (i.e., skeptics or nonpertinent items on the checklist) to rule out alternative explanations.

In another study, in which controls were used, Schmeidler worked with her colleague, M. Maher, of the Psychology Department of the City University of New York. They investigated the stories of two family members who reported seeing a ghost. (M. Maher and G. Schmeidler, "Quantitative Investigation of a Recurrent Apparition," *JASPR*, 69 (1975): 341–345.) The investigators provided checklists of descriptive terms for the family to fill out and floor plans to mark showing what appeared to happen and where. Then four sensitives and eight skeptics went through the house individually, having no contact with anyone knowing the details of the case. They each filled out a checklist and floor plan of what they experienced. The results were inconclusive. One sensitive's floor plan resembled that of the witnesses. Only two sensitives filled out the checklist correctly; one of these had significant correspondence with the family checklist. The control subjects (who were skeptics) did not show significant results nor did infrared photographs offer anything other than "normal" explanations. Such attempts at quantitative study often produce results that are noncorroborative.

20. T. Moss and G. Schmeidler, "Quantitative Investigation of a Haunted House with Sensitives and a Control Group," *JASPR*, 62 (October 1968): 399–410. Schmeidler responded to reports of four witnesses about a ghost in Los Angeles. On the basis of the witnesses' reports, a list of descriptive terms was compiled. "Control" descriptive terms were added of items that had not been noted by the witnesses. A floor plan of the house was drawn up and marked by the witnesses. Eight sensitives were allowed to walk through the house, accompanied by individuals unfamiliar with the case. Three sensitives had significant correspondence with the checklist items given by the witnesses, two of them to a marked degree. Eight control subjects were given the floor plan and checklist, and three of these showed a moderate tendency to mark the pertinent items on the checklist. Neither sensitives nor controls had any results with the floor plan.

21. G. N. M. Tyrrell, *Science and Psychical Phenomena* (New York: Harper Brothers, 1938).

22. For more information see L. Spence, *The Encyclopaedia of Occultism* (New Hyde Park, N. Y.: University Books, 1960; and E. Gross, *The Ouija Board* (Chicago: Moody Press, 1975).

23. W. F. Prince, "The Case of Patience Worth: A Critical Study of Certain Unusual Phenomena," *Boston Society of Psychical Research* (1929), p. 8.

24. O. Heller, quoted in I. Litvag, *Singer in the Shadows: The Strange Story of Patience Worth* (New York: Macmillan, 1972), 257.

25. W. F. Prince, "The Case of Patience Worth," p. 9.

26. For further information, see O. LeRoy, *Levitation* (London, 1928); H. Carrington, *Higher Psychical Development* (New York: Dodd, Mead, 1924); and N. Fodor, *The Encyclopaedia of Psychic Science* (London: Arthurs Press, 1933).

27. W. Crookes, *Researches in the Phenomena of Spiritualism* (London: John Burns, n. d.).

28. A. Dubrov, "Biogravitation and Psychotronics," *The Journal of Impact of Science on Society* (UNESCO), 24, 4 (October–December 1974): 311–319.

29. E. R. Dodds, "Supernormal Phenomena in Classical Antiquity."

30. For further information, see A. C. Doyle, *History of Spiritualism* (London: Cassell, 1926)

Two additional tests have been recently conducted of the possible source of information received by mediums. The first was by Karlis Osis of the American Society for Psychical Research (Osis, "Linkage Experiments with Mediums," *JASPR*, 60 (1966): 91–125). Osis conducted three studies to attempt to determine whether a medium receives information from psi contact with the deceased or from psi contact with the survivors who serve as verifiers of the information received. Two or three intermediaries were placed between the mediums and the verifiers to serve as barriers. An "appointments medium," allegedly in contact with the deceased, set a time at which the other mediums were to contact the deceased, and also devised signals for them to use to call him. No strong evidence of possible psi communication with either the deceased or the verifiers was found.

The second test was by Ian Stevenson of the Department of Parapsychology at the University of Virginia Medical School (Stevenson, "A Communicator Unknown to Medium and Sitters," *JASPR*, 64 (1970): 53–65). Through a medium, Stevenson observed a case of a phenomenon known as a "drop-in communicator." Such a communicator, previously unknown to either medium or sitters, allegedly appears as an unexpected control in a mediumistic session. In the case described, the communicator gave details about his alleged past life, most of which were later verified to the satisfaction of the investigator.

31. E. Coly, personal communication with the authors, May 12, 1977.

32. I. Progoff, *Image of an Oracle* (New York: Helix, 1964), p. 2.

33. A. Angoff, *Eileen Garrett and the World Beyond the Senses* (New York: Morrow, 1974), pp. 177–186.

34. M. Ryzl, *Parapsychology: A Scientific Approach* (New York: Hawthorn, 1970), p. 46. A related experiment was done to determine the accuracy of an alleged medium by W. G. Roll, at the Psychical Research Foundation in Durham, North Carolina (Roll, "Free Verbal Response and Identi-Kit Tests with a Medium," *JASPR*, 65 (1971): 185–191). Roll studied a man named Herbert Beyer, who gave mediumistic readings to seven women and seven men. The men and women were four feet away from Beyer, facing him, but in another room. The experimenters kept Beyer sensorially isolated from the people. A "blind" experimenter worked with Beyer, and another with the targets. Transcripts of all the readings of people of the same sex were given to the targets, and they rated each statement as to how it applied to them. Beyer also used an Identi-Kit to arrange a composite of facial features for each target person. Results of both procedures were positive, but not statistically significant.

35. For further information on reincarnation, see T. Bestermann, *Collected Papers on the Paranormal* (New York: Grier Garrett, 1968).

36. I. Stevenson, "Some New Cases Suggestive of Reincarnation. II. The Case of Bishen Chand," *JASPR*, 66 (October 1972): 375–400.

37. Stevenson, "Some New Cases," p. 393.

38. Stevenson, "Some New Cases," p. 400.

39. C. Tart, "Concerning the Scientific Study of the Human Aura," *Journal of the Society for Psychical Research*, 46, 75 (March 1972).

40. S. Karagulla, *Breakthrough to Creativity* (Santa Monica, Calif.: DeVorss, 1967), pp. 158–159.

41. M. Gauquelin, *The Scientific Basis of Astrology, Myth or Reality* (New York: Stein and Day, 1969).

42. L. Rubin and C. Honorton, "Separating the Yins From the Yangs," *Proceedings of the Parapsychological Association*, 8 (1971), pp. 6–7.

43. J. B. Rhine and J. G. Pratt, *Parapsychology: Frontier Science of the Mind* (Springfield, Ill.: Thomas, 1957).

12. Some New Interests

1. B. Brown, *New Mind, New Body* (New York: Harper & Row, 1974), p. 406.

2. T. Budzynski, personal conversation with Jim Hickman, technical director, Psi SEARCH exhibit, October 1974.

3. J. B. Rhine, personal communication with the authors, January 1977.

4. S. D. Kirlian and V. Kh. Kirlian, "Photography and Visual Observations by Means of High-Frequency Currents," *Journal of Scientific and Applied Photography,* 6 (1961): 397–403.

5. W. A. Tiller, "Are Psychoenergetic Pictures Possible?" *New Scientist* (April 25, 1974): 160–163.

6. J. Hubacher and T. Moss, "The Phantom Leaf Effect as Revealed Through Kirlian Photography," *Psychoenergetic Systems,* 1 (1976): 223–232.

7. W. A. Tiller, "Are Psychoenergetic Pictures Possible?"; and D. I. Boyers and W. A. Tiller, "Corona Discharge Photography," *Journal of Applied Physics,* 44 (1973): 3102–3112.

8. Tiller, "Are Psychoenergetic Pictures Possible?" p. 163.

9. J. O. Pehek, H. J. Kyler, and D. L. Faust, "Image Modulation in Corona Discharge Photography," *Science,* 194 (1976): 263–270.

10. E. D. Dean, "High-Voltage Radiation Photography of a Healer's Finger," in S. Krippner and D. Rubin (eds.), *The Kirlian Aura* (New York: Doubleday, 1974), pp. 80–84.

11. H. E. Montandon, "Psychophysiological Aspects of the Kirlian Phenomenon: A Confirmatory Study," *JASPR,* 71 (1977): 45–53.

12. Boyers and Tiller, "Corona Discharge Photography."

13. D. Rubin and S. Krippner, "The Cosmic Flow," in Krippner and Rubin (eds.), *The Kirlian Aura* (New York: Doubleday, 1974), pp. 17–23.

14. J. C. Bose, *Growth and Tropic Movements of Plants* (New York: Longmans-Green, 1929).

15. C. Backster, "Evidence of Primary Perception in Plant Life," *International Journal of Parapsychology,* 10 (Winter 1968): 329–348.

16. K. A. Horowitz, D. C. Lewis, and E. L. Gasteiger, "Plant 'Primary Perception': Electrophysiological Unresponsiveness to Brine Shrimp Killing," *Science,* 189 (1975): 478–480. The experimenters attempted to confirm evidence offered by Cleve Backster suggestive of sensitivity in plants. They followed his procedure in five experiments, each of which involved responses from four philodendrons, but were unable to duplicate Backster's findings.

17. R. V. Johnson, Letter to the editor, *Journal of Parapsychology,* 36 (1972): 71–72. Johnson could not obtain Backster's effect of plant response to brine shrimp death in a carefully controlled environment. He found no reaction in plants he tested. He suggests that temperature and humidity fluctuations might account for Backster's results. This possibility cannot be eliminated, since Backster provided no details about temperature in his report.

18. J. Kmetz, "A Study of Primary Perception in Plant and Animal Life," *JASPR,* 71 (1977): 157–170.

19. See H. Thurston, *Ghosts and Poltergeists* (Chicago: Gateway, 1954) for more information.

20. See A. Evian, *The Mediumship of Maria Silbert* (London: Rider, 1936) for more information.

21. W. E. Cox, "Some Experiments with Uri Geller," *Journal of Parapsychology,* 38 (December 1974): 408–411.

22. R. H. Thouless, *From Anecdote to Experiment in Psychical Research* (London: Routledge and Kegan Paul, 1972), pp. 144–145.

23. J. G. Pratt and H. H. J. Keil, "Firsthand Observations of Nina S. Kulagina Suggestive of PK Upon Static Objects," *JASPR,* 67 (October 1973): 381–390.

24. For further information, see D. Scott Rogo, "Photographs by the Mind, A Brief History of a Controversial Subject," *Psychic Magazine* (April 1970): 40–46.

25. J. Eisenbud, "Two Camera and Television Experiments with Ted Serios," *JASPR,* 64 (1970): 261–276. In a session at a TV studio, Serios produced eleven images with the videotape, none related to the target. Serios holds a paper tube, 1½ in. x 1 in., while making his attempts, which he rolls in front of the experimenters and permits them to examine at any time. His results, especially with the videotape and lensless camera, would require a complex apparatus to fake.

26. I. Stevenson and J. G. Pratt, "Exploratory Investigations of the Psychic Photography of Ted Serios," *JASPR,* 62 (April, 1968): 103–129; and "Further Investigations of the Psychic Photography of Ted Serios," *JASPR,* 63 (October, 1969): 352–364. Tight controls were maintained over the Polaroid cameras, the film, and Serios' tube of paper. In the second of these two tests, elaborate surveillance procedures for the tube of paper were introduced. A few blackies, one image, and several other conceivably abnormal prints were obtained in many trials. The results, although not as strong as in previous tests, were considered significant because the experimenters believed any possible means of fraud were eliminated. The results seem to confirm what Jule Eisenbud had found in Denver with the same subject.

27. J. G. Pratt, *ESP Research Today: A Study of Developments in Parapsychology Since 1960* (Metuchen, N.J.: Scarecrow, 1973), p. 114.

28. W. Roll, *Theta, The Journal of the Psychical Research Foundation, Inc.,* 4, 3 (Summer 1976): 18.

29. Elisabeth Kubler-Ross presentation to Holistic Health Conference, San Diego, California, September 5, 1976.

30. R. Moody, *Life After Life* (New York: Bantam, 1975).

31. A. Nietzke, "The Miracle of Kubler-Ross," *Human Behavior* (September 1977): 22.

32. W. James, *The Principles of Psychology,* (New York: Henry Holte, 1890).

33. M. Ferguson, "An Editorial," *Brain Mind Bulletin* (July 4, 1977): 1.

34. R. E. Ornstein, ed., *The Nature of Human Consciousness* (San Francisco: W. H. Freeman, 1973): xi.

35. C. Tart, personal communication with the authors, October 14, 1977.

36. C. Tart, *Psi: Scientific Studies of the Psychic Realm* (New York: Dutton, 1977), p. 213.

37. J. Vallee, *The Invisible College* (New York: Dutton, 1975), p. 20.

38. J. A. Hynek, *The UFO Experience* (New York: Ballantine, 1974).

39. Survey by Dr. Peter Sturrock, Professor of Astrophysics, as described in a Stanford News Service release, March 15, 1976.

40. A. R. G. Owen, *Psychic Mysteries of the North* (New York: Harper & Row, 1975).

41. E. L. Smith, "The Raudive Voice: Objective or Subjective? A Discussion," *JASPR,* 68 (1974): 91–100.

13. Possible Applications of Psi

1. J. B. Rhine, *New World of the Mind* (New York: Sloane, 1953), p. 251.

2. Psi SEARCH Exhibit.

3. Psi SEARCH Exhibit.

4. J. Swift, *Gulliver's Travels* (London: J. M. Dent and Co., 1896), p. 212.

5. M. Davidson (ed.), *Astronomy for Every Man* (New York: Dutton, 1953), as quoted in Psi SEARCH.

6. B. Smith, personal communication with Jim Hickman, Psi SEARCH technical director, September 1974.

7. See I. Stevenson, "A Review and Analysis of Paranormal Experiences Connected with the Sinking of the Titanic," *JASPR*, 54 (October, 1960).

8. T. Moss, "ESP Effects in 'Artists' Contrasted with 'Non-Artists'," *Journal of Parapsychology*, 3 (1969): 57–69. Moss compared the psi performance of a group of artists (writers, actors, composers, painters, etc.) with that of a group of nonartists (engineers, teachers, housewives, etc.). The senders were isolated from the subjects and tried to project an image of a photographic slide by means of psi. Artists scored significantly higher than nonartists in identifying the target slide.

9. T. Moss and J. A. Gengerelli, "Telepathy and Emotional Stimuli: A Controlled Experiment," *Journal of Abnormal Psychology*, 72 (1967): 341–348. This experiment was designed to use emotionally charged stimuli as the focus of psi tests. The sender concentrated on emotionally arousing slides while listening to appropriate music. Psi results were extremely strong in those cases where the sender and/or the subject were artists.

10. C. Honorton, "Creativity and Precognitive Scoring Level," *Journal of Parapsychology*, 31 (1967): 29–42.

11. "Profiles in Business," *Psychic Magazine*, 6, 1 (December 1974): 29.

12. "Profiles in Business," p. 30.

13. E. D. Dean, J. Mihalasky, S. Ostrander, and L. Schroeder, *Executive ESP* (New York: Prentice Hall, 1974), pp. 230–233. Dean and Mihalasky investigated the possible link between psi and the "hunches" of successful executives. Twenty groups of business managers were given computer-scored tests of precognition, and also tests for dynamic or non-dynamic personality traits (dynamism was believed to be related to success in business). In sixteen out of twenty groups, the dynamic managers scored higher in their ability to predict the future. Two groups of company presidents were also given precognition tests, and their scores were compared with their companies' profit records from the last five years. Again, the more successful executives did better at predicting the future.

14. S. Marvinney, "The Ancient Art of Dowsing," *The Conservationist*, 29, 1 (August–September 1974).

15. Letter from R. C. Willey, Secretary of the American Society of Dowsers, to the authors, June 30, 1976.

16. K. L. Roberts, *Henry Gross and His Dowsing Rod* (New York: Doubleday, 1951).

17. J. B. Rhine, "Some Exploratory Tests in Dowsing," *Journal of Parapsychology*, 11 (1947): 175–190; also R. J. Cadoret, "The Reliable Application of ESP," *Journal of Parapsychology*, 19 (1955): 203–227. D. G. Chadwick and L. Jensen of the University of Utah made an objective evaluation of dowsing ability for the U.S. Geological Survey. They used a 100-square-yard area for their study. One hundred and fifty subjects dowsed the area, and markers were put down wherever they got a dowsing reaction. The area was then analyzed for variations in the natural magnetic field of the earth. The results showed a significant relation between the dowsers' reactions and the magnetic field variations.

18. K. Osis, "Some Explorations with Dowsing Techniques," *JASpr*, 54 (1960): 141–152.

19. Z. Harvalik, "A Biophysical Magnetometer Gradiometer," *Journal of the Virginia Academy of Science*, 21, 2 (1970):

59. Harvalik attempted to determine whether or not there is a physiological basis for dowsing. He created artificial magnetic fields by placing electrodes in damp soil and passing magnetic current between them. Fifty-four dowsers held rods above these weak fields, and forty-three responded to the fields. After several practice trials, five more responded. Apparently people have the ability to detect weak magnetic fields by the skillful manipulation of dowsing rods.

20. F. B. Bond, *The Gate of Remembrance* (Oxford: B. H. Blackwell, 1920).

21. J. Goodman, "Psychic Archaeology: Methodology and the Empirical Evidence from Flagstaff, Arizona," paper presented at a Symposium on Parapsychology and Anthropology, 1974 American Anthropological Association convention.

22. N. J. Emerson, "Clairvoyance and Archaeological Fieldwork: Evidence from Canada, Mexico, and England," paper presented at a Symposium on Parapsychology and Anthropology, 1974 American Anthropological Association convention.

23. Emerson, "Clairvoyance," p. 9.

24. J. H. Pollack, *Croiset the Clairvoyant* (Garden City, N.Y.: Doubleday, 1964), p. 129.

25. As quoted in *Harper's*, November 1959, p. 41.

26. As quoted in R. Targ and H. Puthoff, *Mind Reach* (New York: Delacorte, 1977), p. 47.

27. The address is Box 482, Times Square Station, New York, N.Y.

28. M. Anderson and R. White, "ESP Score Level in Relation to Students' Attitude Toward Teacher-Agents Acting Simultaneously," *Journal of Parapsychology*, 22 (1958): 20–28. In these tests of the relationship between students' psi performance and their attitudes toward their teachers, the students were asked to guess the order of five Zener card ESP symbols in randomly selected target lists in sealed manila envelopes. Both teachers and students then rated their feelings about each other on questionnaires.

29. G. Jampolsky and M. E. Haight, "A Pilot Study of ESP in Hyperkinetic Children," in J. D. Morris et al. (eds.), *Research in Parapsychology 1974* (Metuchen, N. J.: Scarecrow, 1975): 13–15. In related experiments, J. G. van Busschbach attempted to determine whether younger or older children would do better on ESP tests. (J. G. van Busschbach, "An Investigation of ESP in First and Second Grades in American Schools," *Journal of Parapsychology*, 25 (1961): 161–174; and J. G. van Busschbach, "An Investigation of ESP in First and Second Grades of Dutch Schools," *Journal of Parapsychology*, 23 (1959): 227–237.) He did nine different psi studies with school children in Holland and America. Several kinds of simple targets, including words and colors, were used. The teacher, at the rear of the classroom behind a screen, served as sender. In both countries, children in grades 1–7 showed strong psi abilities, and children in grades 7–12 scored slightly below what would be expected by chance. No implications were suggested about the apparent ability of younger children to do better at ESP tasks.

30. E. Shields, "Comparison of Children's Guessing Ability (ESP) with Personality Characteristics," *Journal of Parapsychology*, 26, 3 (September 1962): 200–210. Shields administered the psi tests disguised as "guessing tests" to ninety-eight public school children who had been referred to her for help with behavioral, learning, or emotional problems. They were also given personality and intelligence tests.

31. Shields, "Comparison,"

32. M. Johnson, "A Written Academic Exam as a Disguised

Test of Clairvoyance," in W. G. Roll et al. (eds.), *Research in Parapsychology 1972* (Metuchen, N. J.: Scarecrow, 1973): 28–30.

33. F. K. Paddock, personal communication with the authors, May 18, 1977.

34. C. Simonton, "The Role of the Mind in Cancer Therapy," in S. R. Dean (ed.), *Psychiatry and Mysticism* (Chicago: Nelson-Hall, 1975), pp. 293–308.

35. S. Krippner, personal communication with the authors, October 27, 1976.

36. See, for example, E. Hilgard, *The Experience of Hypnosis* (New York: Harcourt, Brace & World, 1965).

37. S. Krippner and A. Villoldo, *The Realms of Healing* (Millbrae, Calif.: Celestial Arts, 1976), pp. 1–24.

38. S. Hammond, *We Are All Healers* (New York: Harper & Row, 1973).

39. R. Van de Castle, "An Investigation of Psi Abilities Among the Cuna Indians of Panama," *Proceedings of an International Conference: Parapsychology and Anthropology* (New York: Parapsychology Foundation, 1973), pp. 80–97.

40. J. Dick and R. Bergman, National Institute of Mental Health Program Reports No. 5 (Rockville, Maryland: Department of Health, Education, and Welfare, 1971).

41. H. Stewart et al., "Kindling of Hope in the Disadvantaged: A Study of the Afro-American Healers," *Mental Hygiene*, 55 (1971): 96–100. Stewart studied Afro-American healers practicing in a Georgia county. Among those interviewed was Ma Sue, aged nearly 100, who had practiced laying-on-of-hands, prayer, and suggestion. She concluded that faith on the part of both the healer and the healed was essential if the treatment was to succeed.

42. R. Katz, "Education for Transcendence: Lessons from the ¡Kung Zhu/Twasi," *Journal of Transpersonal Psychology*, 5 (1973): 136–155. Instead of training one special person to become a healer, the ¡Kung teach all of their young men a special dance, in which they go into altered states of consciousness and attempt to cure ailing members of the tribe.

43. D. J. West, *Eleven Lourdes Miracles* (New York: Garrett/Helix, 1957).

44. H. L. Cayce (ed.), *The Edgar Cayce Reader* (New York: Warner, 1969), p. 8.

45. For further information, see T. Sugrue, *There is a River* (New York: Holt, 1956), a biography of Cayce.

46. L. LeShan, *The Medium, The Mystic, and The Physicist* (New York: Viking, 1974), pp. 105–112.

47. B. Grad, "Some Biological Effects of 'Laying on of Hands': A Review of Experiments with Animals and Plants," *JASPR*, 59 (1965): 95–127.

48. Grad, "Some Biological Effects."

49. M. J. Smith, "Paranormal Effects on Enzyme Activity," *Proceedings of the Parapsychological Association*, 5 (1968): 15–16.

50. D. Krieger, "Healing by the 'Laying on of Hands' as a Facilitator of Bioenergetic Change: The Response of In-Vivo Human Hemoglobin," *Psychoenergetic Systems*, 3 (1975).

51. D. Krieger, "A Second Experiment in 'Laying-on-of-Hands'", *Psychoenergetic Systems*, 7 (1976).

52. East West Academy of Healing Arts, Council of Nurse-Healers, 33 Ora Way, San Francisco, CA 94131.

53. G. Watkins and A. Watkins, "Possible PK Influence on the Resuscitation of Anesthetized Mice," *Journal of Parapsychology*, 35 (1971): 257–272.

54. R. Wells and J. Klein, "A Replication of a 'Psychic Healing' Paradigm," *Journal of Parapsychology*, 36 (1972).

55. C. D. Broad, in J. M. O. Wheatley and H. L. Edge (eds.), *Philosophical Dimensions of Parapsychology* (Springfield, Ill.: Thomas, 1976), p. 20.

56. H. H. Price, in J. R. Smythies (ed.), *Science and ESP* (New York: Humanities, 1967), p. 42.

57. J. Palmer and M. Dennis, "A Community Mail Survey of Psychic Experiences," in J. D. Morris et al. (eds.), *Research in Parapsychology, 1974* (Metuchen, N. J.: Scarecrow, 1975): 130–133.

58. Professor Sidgwick Committee, "Report on the Census of Hallucinations," *Proceedings of the Society of Psychical Research*, 10 (1894): 25–422.

59. L. E. Rhine, "Frequency of Types of Experiences in Spontaneous Precognition," *Journal of Parapsychology*, 18, 2 (1954): 93–123.

60. L. E. Rhine, "Subjective Forms of Spontaneous Psi Experiences," *Journal of Parapsychology*, 17, 1 (1953): 79–114.

61. R. Stanford, "An Experimentally Testable Model for Spontaneous Psi Events: I. Extrasensory Events," *JASPR*, 68 (1974): 34–57.

62. Stanford, "An Experimentally Testable Model," p. 54. Stanford uses the phrase "Psi-Mediated Instrumental Response" to describe the way in which he thinks psi may become a part of daily occurrences.

14.   Breaking the Circle

1. R. H. Thouless, *From Anecdote to Experiment in Psychical Research* (London: Routledge and Kegan Paul, 1972), p. 32.

2. *Psi Lines: A Documentation of the Psi SEARCH Exhibition*, (Los Angeles: Psi SEARCH Institute, 1975), p. 32.

3. A. Ochsner, personal communication with the authors, February 12, 1977.

Index